ME WITHOUT HIM

an ablative mood

Henry 磊磊 Roark

Weather Pattern Press

ISBN: 979-8-9971120-0-4

Published by Weather Pattern Press.
henryroark.com/weather-pattern-press

To all who light my way in darkness,
and LCD, my tiny ghost who haunts me still.

Contents

Author's Note

When new potential readers see my book's subtitle, I'm often asked what *ablative* means. The ablative is a grammatical noun case, most commonly found in Latin, but also Sanskrit, for relations between words meaning *away from* or *by/with* or simply *leaving* with distance and departure. Many modern languages handle these kinds of relations with just prepositions.

I'm using the ablative here with artistic license to establish the mood of the entire collection. In grammar, a case marks a noun's relation to other words in the sentence, whereas a mood marks a verb's relation to reality along with its emotional register. A sentence can hold the same facts, yet change the grammatical mood, and the feeling and tenor of the narrative shifts.

> The indicative says this happened, *he left*.
> The subjunctive says this might have, or didn't, or I wish it had,
> *if only I had told him.*
> The conditional relies on another contingency,
> *I would have told him, had he asked.*
> The imperative makes demands, *come back.*
> The optative expresses wishes and hopes,
> *would that he had stayed*.

You might guess that I never live in the indicative. Recently, when asked what register I write in, I replied *haunting*—what I meant was I hoped to have lasting or impactful resonance. When asked again what I saw my writing as metaphorically, I replied *a beacon* and sometimes, *a flare*.

I hope this collection speaks to anyone who needs a reminder, you are not alone. All of us hope, all of us love, all of us suffer, all of us endure, all of us live, all of us die, all of us dream—to borrow from *All of Strangers* (2023).

I who have known the ablative as absence, abandonment, an action done to me, write as a beacon, a flare, a memorial.

Henry 磊磊 Roark
August 2026

I. A Story

⌈Horror is the truth about abstraction. ...Sublimity is considered superior precisely because it need not engage the faculties of persuasion. It is a *sensation*; when the sublime strikes, like pain or mortal fear, we simply *know* it to be true.⌋

Comaroff & Ong, *Horror in Architecture*

Host

Chapter One: Limbic Residency, Stage III

The problem with grief, Oliver had learned, was that it had excellent taste in real estate.

It had moved into the left side of his rib cage sometime last fall, between the week when he proposed and when Callum responded with whatever he said, which for all intents and purposes was not a *yes*; and over the following days, slid to a *no*. Grief toured the neighborhood inside his chest, liked the lighting, and signed a lease without his consent, let alone discussing it with him. By the time Oliver realized what happened, it had settled in.

This was San Francisco, so of course someone eventually built a product, or *grief tolerance as a service* (GTaaS), for this situation. The science had been there for years: attachment theory, limbic imprinting, the discovery that love and grief were physical events encoded in the amygdala and hippocampus, not only felt but measurable: structures older than language and faster than thought, sitting beneath the reasoning brain and indifferent to it. It felt before you understood, bonded before you decided to. When traumatic separation occurred, it left measurable traces, imprints that persisted long after the conscious mind had moved on, or tried to.

It took a minimum viable product, a Series B, and a team in SoMa to turn it into a billable service. The Remnant Assessment Clinic (RAC) opened on Market Street four years ago, backed by the same capital disrupting every other aspect of lived experience, offering what their intake materials called a "clinically validated framework for post-attachment limbic integration."

The form Oliver filled out called it Limbic Residency, Stage I. The clinician who explained it to him, Dr. Osei, seemed mildly apologetic about the whole matter and said it was more common than most people understood. Many didn't even realize they had it, before it dissolved and integrated on its own. For the other progressed cases like Oliver's, with the right support, most patients found it manageable.

Manageable, Oliver repeated, in a whisper to himself.

That was one word for it. He'd been managing for three years. He was excellent at management. He managed through the first winter, which was the worst, and the second spring, which was worse in a different way: the cruelty of seasons continuing, trees dressing and undressing, birds leaving and returning with complete indifference. The world moved on without him. He managed with Al-Anon meetings in churches, sessions with his therapist, Dr. Lim, who had a talent for asking questions he was avoiding, in the tone of a professional who had all day to wait in uncomfortable silence. He managed by burning garden sage at every location in the East Bay that carried a memory, which turned out to include most of Oakland and Berkeley. He was willing to try any recommendation.

What sent him to the clinic happened a year after Callum left, on a Thursday evening in Temescal, Oakland. He hadn't decided to follow him. That was what he told Derek afterward, and how he explained it to Dr. Lim, and what he kept telling himself during the twenty minutes he sat outside the nearby laundromat afterward: it wasn't a conscious choice. One moment he was walking north on Telegraph, the next his legs pulled toward a man half a block ahead and was closing the distance without instruction. Each step felt like confirmation. The pull in his chest, recognizing the tilt of his head, the height, the way his hands moved when he walked—felt different now: less weather, more current.

The silhouette turned to walk into an apartment building. The main door was still swinging when Oliver reached it. He caught it and went in. He followed him up a half-flight of stairs and through an open apartment door before the word *wrong* started flashing with warning lights in his mind. By then it was too late. He was standing in someone else's entryway with someone else's art on the walls and someone else's plants throughout, and a stranger turning around to face him with an expression that started as surprise, but hadn't yet decided what to become.

Four seconds. Maybe five. Oliver standing in Derek's entryway piecing together that he had followed a stranger into his home because the dull throbbing in his left ribs matched the man's profile to Callum, and his body had responded before his conscious mind could intervene.

He wasn't sure what his face was doing during those five seconds, but he hoped it conveyed horror at his own actions. He apologized profusely. He considered turning around instantly and making a run for it. Derek, whose name he learned because Derek introduced himself in his own home to a stranger who had forced entry; he adopted the instinctive politeness of a host attempting to tone down a frightening social situation into a manageable one. Perhaps he had experience entertaining unpleasant characters he didn't personally like. Either way, he handled it with more grace than Oliver deserved. Oliver trudged back down the stairs, still horrified, and out onto Telegraph to a bench outside a closed laundromat. He held his head in his hands, crouched over, and did not move for twenty minutes as he practiced the breathwork he was taught.

He built a story around it. Not a lie—the facts were the facts: wrong apartment, wrong person, fractured apology for an unforgivable trespass. But by the time he stood up, he had spun it into a story he could tell himself and others. The incident was evidence of his progressing prosopagnosia, more commonly known as face-blindness. The prosopagnosia was a fully understandable medical condition and explanation. He made it inside someone else's home before his brain's alarm bells kicked in. He was stable, though. He knew what delusional looked like for him, along with psychotic, at least in the aftermath. And this wasn't either. He would tell Dr. Lim the sanitized version. He always did, and it always held.

He looked up the clinic that night. The language on the intake page confirmed what he always suspected: loving someone long enough and hard enough left a physical scar in the limbic system, measurable and diagnosable, with treatment options. He didn't completely understand how limbic imprinting, post-attachment neurological integration, remnants left by traumatic separation worked, but it mapped onto what had been happening to him in a way that ordinary grief literature hadn't.

He made an appointment for the following week.

The Stage I diagnosis had come shortly after. Dr. Osei had been matter-of-fact about it: early-stage residencies resolved on their own in most cases. The limbic system metabolizes the remnant the way it metabolized other acute traumas, unevenly but eventually. She recommended therapy, the Al-Anon meetings Oliver was already attending, and a check-in at six months.

The six-month check-in showed the limbic residency had progressed to Stage II. The remnant had grown and organized. It developed a center of mass, a coherent network structure, and a signal the scanner could now locate and measure. Dr. Osei suggested pharmacological suppression to reduce the signal and act as containment. Oliver remained resistant and was frankly embarrassed the limbic residency and remnant had organized to this degree.

Now he understood that this was the remnant at work. Stage II was when it had learned to speak in the vocabulary of his own recovery, white-knuckling, doing the work, sitting with discomfort rather than medicating around it—and used it to keep him in place. Declining the drug suppression felt like choosing integrity.

He spent the following eighteen months watching himself grow more desperate. The sage burning, which started as a single visit to Willard Park, became a circuit: five locations, then seven, then twelve, each one added because the previous ones hadn't worked, each addition feeling like commitment, or a sunk cost fallacy, rather than escalation. The letters to Callum, which Dr. Lim had suggested as a bounded practice, became nightly, and the primary place Oliver processed anything. The ring, discovered in Marin, arrived on his finger and stayed there with a logic he couldn't quite reconstruct when he tried. He told himself he was moving through it.

The follow-up appointment was a year later. He filled out the new intake form in the waiting room as quickly as possible without looking up. After the scans, the results came back: Stage III, Elevated Consolidation. *Intervention review recommended.*

Oliver had mixed feelings seeing Dr. Osei again. The appointment was brief, or tried to be. Dr. Osei aspirationally scheduled fifteen-minute slots and routinely ran over them, not from inefficiency but from delivering emotionally ambiguous news and how patients would receive it. *She should really try adding a five-minute buffer*, Oliver thought, as he once again wanted to fix problems with solutions nobody asked for.

"Stage III presents differently," she said, pulling the scan results onto the screen beside her desk and turning it toward him. "I want to show you what we're looking at."

Oliver looked.

He saw the scans at his Stage I appointment. Stage I looked like misty weather on the edge of a radar image, a diffuse low-pressure system at the periphery, shaped enough to be diagnosed as limbic residency, loose enough to seem manageable, at least to him. Stage II had a defined center of mass, a coherent mesh network covering his limbic like a differently textured concrete foundation poured over the original.

Stage III looked stranger.

The remnant on the screen was no longer sitting on top of his limbic structures the way it had at Stage II, a defined mass with visible edges. It had burrowed and spread into them, denser at the core, darker on the scan, dissolved boundaries between remnant and his own tissue, whereas at Stage II they had been clean. It was woven through now, structurally fused together. It looked less like an intrusion than original construction, except Oliver knew his own floor plan, and this wasn't it.

It felt particularly dense at the center, where Oliver felt it as chest and rib pressure every morning. It had also reached into the prefrontal cortex, the part of the brain responsible for executive functioning and reasoning, Dr. Osei explained, what he used to think his way through, not that it had worked. The remnant even threaded itself into his sleep cycles, which would normally degrade it over time, and was why he hadn't slept past four in the morning in three years.

The only analogous situation Oliver could think of was when he had a tooth infection he couldn't feel for over two years. He'd noticed some mild irritation, assumed his wisdom teeth were finally coming in like his dentist had been warning him about for years, and booked an appointment. The oral surgeon looked in his mouth, examined the x-ray, and said he was surprised Oliver came in without screaming in agony. The infection had been ravaging for a couple years, he estimated. It had found a crack in the tooth, killed the nerve endings, and made itself comfortable while Oliver couldn't tell anything was amiss. In that regard, it was a perfect parasite. Another few months and it would have breached the sinus canal, leading to a thin membrane with the brain. He needed the molar out, the infection flushed, and the wisdom teeth removed.

Without his left molar, Oliver thought the only redeeming aspect was that his body would be easily identifiable in case of murder, even after heavy decomposition.

"The scanner can see it," Dr. Osei said, "but can no longer cleanly read it as separate from you."

She said it with clinical neutrality, describing a biological process, which it was, but also just felt like poor bedside manners. Oliver did not love progressing from Stage I to Stage III under her care.

"The false matches," he said. "When I see him in strangers. That's the remnant using the prosopagnosia?"

"Consistent with Stage III," she said. "Every false match acts as a feeding event. His face is encoded so deeply that your brain keeps finding it in strangers, and every time it does, the remnant grows off the emotional pattern in your limbic system. Think of it like agar in a petri dish. You've been providing the exact conditions for sustaining it. It's been running that cycle for some time."

Oliver absorbed this. He wanted to blame her, yell, demand why none of her recommendations had prevented the progression. His prosopagnosia hadn't just made him vulnerable; it had given the remnant air cover and a feeding mechanism. A broken, all-you-can-eat filing system the remnant had learned to rifle through at will. It was also why he had progressed to Stage III rather than resolving at Stage II: a limbic system that couldn't reliably release faces couldn't reliably release a remnant either. But Dr. Osei knew about his pre-existing conditions. Or should have.

"Most patients at this stage opt for continued integration rather than intervention," Dr. Osei said, which was clinical speak for: most people decide to let the other person live in them forever, because the alternative requires a surgical extraction on a level they're not ready for.

"What's the intervention?" Oliver asked.

She hesitated, hoping he wouldn't ask. "There are two pathways. We can still try pharmacological suppression. Again, it doesn't remove the remnant, but it contains it and reduces its signal. Most patients find it effective for day-to-day functioning."

"And the other?"

She hesitated again. "Structural excision. It's not a procedure we perform here."

"Where do you perform it?"

"We don't," she said. "It's not covered within our scope. It's not—it's not a procedure the clinic is equipped for."

She said *not covered* like it involved a higher matter beyond insurance coverage or payment. *Ethics?* Oliver wondered. He had a talent for his line of work in architecture, which also extended into the metaphorical. He didn't need to see people's facial expressions to understand how they were feeling or what they were thinking, unlike a branch of design philosophy, *architecture parlante*, that argued exterior design should explicitly reflect the function and purpose of the interior. He knew well enough how people said one line when they meant another all the time.

You can never trust a façade at face value, as one of his professors liked to say. His favorite conceptual designs were Giovanni Piranesi's *Imaginary Prisons* from the 1700s. While they were imaginary only in the sense they could never be built, they revealed more than any of the few façades Piranesi actually did build. And lent themselves well to seeing the inner workings of one man's mind. Oliver looked at the scan. *This is what three years of Callum looks like inside my mind*, he thought, a Piranesi prison: elaborate, shadowed in chiaroscuro, staircases leading nowhere, vaulted ceilings built around an absence. He had been designing them long enough to recognize these walls in others. Oliver's talent meant seeing the rooms people built around themselves. Dr. Osei had constructed, in the space of that brief hesitation, a thin but solid stone wall between them. He resisted pushing on it to test its load-bearing weight.

He took the literature she offered, which was printed on slightly off-white, standard brochure paper; the faded color suggested it had once been a brighter, more hopeful white. He walked back down Market in the fog. He didn't ask Dr. Osei if there was a Stage IV.

—

The clinic opened five years ago. Before that, what Oliver had was simply called *not getting over it*. The prescribed treatment then was therapy, time, relocation, and meeting someone new, administered in whatever order and combination until one of them worked. He had tried them all. None was sufficient, which was seen as a character defect. Oliver's will to live was tenuous at times, but his will to not feel miserable was quite strong. According to his friends, his situation was the kind of ailment you could *will* your way out of, if you tried hard enough, if you loved yourself correctly.

He understood. It still didn't help.

He still woke at the same time every morning, before the birds, before even the pre-dawn light made its tentative offer to the sky, with the sensation of a shifting in the left side of his ribs. He conducted his interior checks, essentially a tour repeating *Am I OK?*, with the careful attention of a contractor performing maintenance on a structure he wasn't sure would hold. Perimeter, check. Damage, more, same, or less, those were the only options to remain purposely vague. He didn't think about Callum directly. Thinking about Callum directly was like pressing a bruise, diagnostic—*yep, still hurts*—but not at all productive. He thought around Callum. Along the walls he put up next to Callum's.

He stopped asking whether the obsessive interior checks were him or the remnant. The question was moot. The checking happened every morning either way.

This was partly literal. After the ECT, electroconvulsive therapy, administered eighteen months before Callum, back when the bipolar episodes were severe enough to warrant it—the kind that wore thin whatever kept realities separate, that brought visions vivid enough to compete with waking life, that left him unable to trust his own perception for days afterward—Oliver developed a mild prosopagnosia. More commonly known as face blindness, though the name was misleading. He could see faces. He could draw them with precision himself to verify with others. He saw the same faces, experienced the same reality as others. He just couldn't reliably connect them to the person he knew. It was recognition without identification; the face arrives, the name and context stays just out of reach. The faces from before the treatment were intact, locked in. Everyone since: familiar, slightly blurred, murkily placeable.

He developed workarounds using height, hairstyle, voice. So did the remnant.

That last part he didn't know yet.

—

The apartment was the one place where the question didn't follow him. Callum had been there enough times that the light beaming through the western window in the late afternoon had become one of the times and places Oliver took a detour around in his own home. Oliver lived there longer, and the space eventually took his shape over Callum's. It was his books on the shelves, his plants throughout, and his art on the walls. The photographs with Callum were in a box under the bed, where he couldn't see them but also couldn't bring himself to move further from his person.

The ring he bought was on the windowsill above the kitchen sink, where he could see it while doing dishes. Salvaged koa wood, two carved whale tails that met but didn't fully enclose. He found it in a shop in Marin when he was browsing aimlessly waiting for a friend. He spent twenty minutes in the shop before understanding what he was going to do with it. He bought it because Callum loved identifying trees. He had called Callum *anam ċara* before he called him anything else: soul friend in Irish Gaelic, the Celtic tradition's name for a person whose presence made you feel more fully yourself. He had meant it. He still did. That was the problem. He already knew what the ring meant and refused, for now, to acknowledge how much of a problem that posed. He knew what Dr. Lim would say.

He didn't know then to question whether the decision to get the ring had been his, or whether it had simply felt that way, indistinguishable from the inside, which was precisely how the remnant preferred it.

He dried his hands and looked out at the stretch of sky trying to decide between gray and darker gray. He'd been reading about Olbers' paradox again that morning, the eighteenth-century conundrum he kept returning to like a tongue returning to a sore tooth. Olbers posited if the universe was infinite and uniformly filled with stars, every line of sight should lead to a star. The night sky should be lit ablaze; instead it's dark. The accepted solution, when it came around two hundred years later, was that the universe was expanding faster than light could cross it. The darkness wasn't emptiness. It was light delayed by distance. It was light that hadn't arrived before the universe expanded further.

Oliver remembered a talk by an astrophysicist at the California Academy of Sciences planetarium where she explained that other intelligent life definitively exists in the universe, that's not the question. The question is whether our periods of advancement overlap in both time and space with theirs.

He first read about the paradox eight months after Callum left, during the weeks he still spent evenings looking for explanations that would make the math of it make sense. He didn't find the math nor the sense. He found Olbers instead, whose questioning was the closest line of inquiry: if love is infinite and the person is still out there, why does everything feel like absence?

The birds flew south in October, following the same instinct they always did: *leave what cannot sustain you in search of what can*. They didn't remain faithful to place by necessity. It's kept them alive for millennia as Earth continues its age-old orbit around the sun. They didn't mistake departure for personal failure, just migration patterns, a rhythm of life.

Oliver did. Or part of him did.

Yet he hadn't left.

He sat at his desk with his laptop open. He had a habit, these past three years, of writing to Callum in a document he would never send. He started in the first winter, when the impulse to reach out was at its highest, and his therapist was firm about the wisdom to not act on it. *Write the letter*, Dr. Lim said. *Don't send it.* And Oliver found, to his own mild horror, that the writing helped. It was the only place he could be entirely honest about what he was carrying.

He closed the laptop, picked up his keys, and walked out into the night.

Market Street at 18:30 on a Tuesday showed a city in transition—the office workers still streaming toward Muni and BART, the evening crowd not yet out, the sun's remaining light streaming through when the fog hadn't fully committed, turning everything briefly golden before giving up. Oliver moved through the sidewalks with his usual practiced attention for navigating crowds and reading beyond faces. Height, hair, gait, the specific slouch of how someone held their shoulders. Clothing as context, voice as confirmation.

He was halfway down the block when he saw him.

Tall, dark oversized jacket, the broad set of shoulders Oliver's limbic system recognized before his conscious mind processed anything. The slight forward lean, the deliberate pace of a walker who knew where he was going and wasn't in a hurry about it. His chest compressed into itself, and he felt the compass-needle pull, orienting toward a true north.

He made himself reverify the details like he learned in cognitive behavioral therapy. Wrong shoes, Callum didn't wear that kind, prioritizing practicality above all else. Wrong hair. Wrong gait on closer inspection, the smoothness slightly off.

Not Callum.

He tallied it: another pattern match to a false positive. His brain couldn't hold new faces reliably, so it matched against what it had, and what it had in abundance was Callum: three years of Callum at every angle, distance, and quality of light, encoded before the ECT scrambled the filing system. As far as Oliver understood, the remnant had nothing to do with seeing Callum everywhere. This was the prosopagnosia he was getting used to: seeing contours and filling in the name it had the most data for.

He identified the error and kept moving.

His chest didn't register the message.

—

The Castro Country Club was not a club in any sense the name implied. It was a recovery meeting space in a neighborhood that had been, at various points in its history, a sanctuary, a battleground, a home where people came to live in peace. The meetings happened in the front room with stackable chairs, coffee from the attached coffeeshop serving Peet's, and the attempted cover-up smell of a space that held a great deal of human honesty without enough ventilation to air it out.

Oliver arrived ten minutes early. He ordered a small Major Dickison decaf he didn't want and found a seat in the fourth row, always at the aisle: visible to the room but not in its direct eyeline. He sat along the back wall in his first three attempts at Al-Anon where he could see both exits and leave with ease, which he had—early and often. He sat in the middle row on his fourth. Progress was measurable by row position, apparently.

The meeting opened. The speaker, the readings, the shares all contributed to the agreement of the anonymous gathering to practice vulnerability and honesty inside these walls, but who reverted back to a different frequency as soon as they stepped outside them. Oliver found the rhythm steadying, despite the quiet discomfort, because it was reliable and grew familiar. The same words in the same order, a ritualized container.

Tonight's speaker share came from Renata who spoke about Step One with the hard earned experience of a returning regular: *we admitted we were powerless over others, that our lives had become unmanageable.* She said she used to read powerless as defeat. She reads it now as relief. The distinction took her years to disentangle.

Oliver listened. He heard shares through the filter of wherever he was at the time, which meant tonight he heard: The three years weren't stubbornness. They weren't weakness. The powerlessness wasn't a character defect. It had a name on a scan, a stage number for progressions, and a clinician who was mildly apologetic about delivering it.

After the meeting he stood by the literature absentmindedly perusing the titles more based on the color of their covers. Vicente found him, which was never a coincidence. Vicente had a talent for appearing at the exact moment Oliver most needed to be found and least wanted to admit it. In this way, he was a lot like Dr. Lim: annoying on purpose and good for him.

Vicente was sixty-one, Puerto Rican, a retired electrician who retrained as a hospital chaplain in his fifties, and a *double winner* in recovery. He wore the same four flannel shirts on rotation like a lumberjack bear from the Pacific Northwest. He had sponsored Oliver for the past fourteen months, and their relationship operated on a hard-to-detect wavelength: loose radiations of warmth undergirded by reliability. Vicente would say the same true statement whether Oliver was stable or catastrophic. The true statement was true regardless, and Oliver needed to hear it.

"You want to tell me about the appointment," Vicente said. A statement, notably not a question.

"Stage III," Oliver said.

Vicente looked at him over his coffee. "Which means." Again, a declarative.

"Elevated Consolidation. They want to discuss intervention options."

"What options." Still lacking any intonation indicating a question.

"Pharmacological suppression. Reduces the signal. Doesn't remove the remnant." He paused. "Or structural excision, which they don't perform and won't refer for."

Vicente went quiet in a way Oliver learned to read as processing rather than waiting. The quiet added a slight density to the air, like weights settling onto a balancing scale.

"There's a third option," Vicente said. "One the clinic doesn't know about. Or knows about and won't acknowledge."

Oliver maintained steady eye contact until he continued.

"I know some people," Vicente said. "Turk Street. They've been operating since before the clinic existed. Before any of this had a product name." He paused. "I'm not telling you it's the right call. I'm just telling you it exists."

"What do they do?"

"What the clinic calls structural excision, plus what the clinic can't classify." Vicente took a sip of his coffee. "It worked for me. Forty years ago. Before it had FDA approval, or any agency that wanted jurisdiction."

Oliver took this in. In fourteen months of sponsorship Vicente never once mentioned his own remnant. The information felt offered like a tightly guarded treasure.

"How do I find them?" Oliver asked.

"I'll send you the address," Vicente said. "Her name is Paloma. She doesn't take clients who aren't ready."

"How will she know if I'm ready?"

"She won't," Vicente said. "You tell her the truth, and then she decides."

Oliver turned the ring on his left hand. The two carved tails. The open space between them. Outside, the fog pressed against the windows, never letting residents forget the ocean was close.

He thought about the man earlier on Market. The wrong shoes, the wrong hair, the desire that stayed in his chest even after his brain had moved on. Three years of that gap: the knowing and the wanting running on separate tracks. Underneath each one, the same question he stopped himself from arriving at. If it was just his brain's prosopagnosia matching against what it had the most data for, why did it always feel like more than mistaken identity? Like the remnant knew more than Oliver?

He didn't have an answer. He had a name on Turk Street: Paloma.

"Send me the address," he said.

Vicente nodded. He finished his coffee. The fog pressed up against them.

Chapter Two: Selective Attention

The address came through at 23:14 that night. Oliver was still awake, lying in the dark of his San Francisco apartment in May with the fog fully in and the city outside reduced to its muffled version of itself.

Paloma. 447 Turk. She knows you're coming. —V

Oliver read it twice. Vicente still signed his texts like letters. *Olds*, he thought. He set his phone face-down on the nightstand. He picked it up and read it again.

She knows you're coming implied Vicente had already told her. Which meant Vicente had been planning to give him the address before the meeting, before Oliver asked, before Stage III was even on the table between them. Which meant Vicente had been observing Oliver and reached his own conclusions, the way sponsors did when they had seventeen years on you and a talent for seeing patterns you weren't yet ready to name.

Oliver put the phone down. He looked at the ceiling. He thought about the scan, the dense organized mass of the remnant on Dr. Osei's screen, the roots it had sent into his limbic system, the places where it had become indistinguishable from him. He thought about her voice saying *every false match is a feeding event* and about the ring on his left hand and the question she didn't answer, which was its own answer.

He thought about all the mornings he woke before sunrise and performed the body and mind scan, when he believed it was grief, love, the stubbornness of a person who chose once. He thought about the letters he wrote to Callum and believed were honesty.

He thought: *what if the carrying wasn't entirely mine?*

He didn't sleep for a long time after that. When he did, it was thin, and he woke like clockwork before the birds, wishing he could for once sleep in.

He called Vicente in the late morning, standing at the kitchen sink with the ring on the windowsill where he had put it sometime in the night without registering.

"She knows I'm coming?" Oliver asked.

"She does," Vicente confirmed.

"So you told her before the meeting?"

"I called her two weeks ago," Vicente said. "After you told me about the Stage II results. I told her you weren't ready yet. Last night I told her you were."

Oliver looked at the ring on the windowsill. "How did you know?"

"Because you asked," Vicente said. "People who aren't ready don't ask. They find reasons why the results and their implications don't apply to them."

Oliver took this in. Outside the birds were chirping on, in a May morning when the fog was still pervasive, but thinning at the edges, tentative, as if waiting to see whether the sun would commit to the day.

"What do I need to know before I go?" Oliver asked.

"Tell her the truth," Vicente said. "All of it. She'll know if you're telling the story you tell yourself instead of the truth, and she won't work with you if so."

"What counts as the story you tell yourself?"

"You know," Vicente said. "You've been doing it long enough."

After he hung up, Oliver stood at the sink. He thought about what story he told himself. He had been doing it for three years with such thoroughness that it had become second nature, with its own morning rituals, its own letters, and desperate practices like burning sage. From the inside, the story looked identical to coping. He was not entirely sure where the story ended and the living began, which was perhaps the point Vicente was making, which was possibly also what Stage III meant in practice: the remnant had been telling the story for so long, the distinction had collapsed.

He picked up the ring. Held it, tracing over the two carved tails. He put it back on his left hand.

He went to work.

His office was on Maiden Lane, a narrow pedestrian alley off Union Square, quieter than the surrounding blocks full of shopping, the scale more human, light arriving at angles wider streets didn't permit. He had chosen the office for this lighting and because Frank Lloyd Wright had designed the building a few doors down in 1948, a proto-Guggenheim circle in a city of Victorian rectangles. Oliver wanted to walk past it every day as a reminder that the given conditions of a site were never the final word on what could be built there. He always admired site specificity.

Theirs was a three-person practice: Oliver, Priya, and a part-time project manager, Rhonda, who worked remotely. Small enough that everyone knew which problems belonged to whom.

He was working on a renovation of a Victorian on Liberty whose owners wanted to open up the back of the house without compromising the load-bearing rear wall. The structural problem was clean: the wall had to stay, but the weight it carried could be redistributed through a steel moment frame, creating an opening without removing the support. He had been working on the solution for three days and was close. He could feel the logic assembling as he stopped forcing it and let the building tell him what it needed.

He stared at the drawings for an hour, his mind preoccupied.

The problem was that he kept thinking about the scan. The remnant woven through his limbic system, indistinguishable in places from his own architecture. The clinic could see it but could no longer cleanly separate it from him, which was why Dr. Osei had said *not a procedure we perform here* with that quality of professional regret that meant: not a procedure anyone licensed would touch.

He looked at the Liberty St drawings. The load-bearing wall. The weight distributed through the structure, essential to the building's integrity and also the obstacle to the opening the owners wanted. You couldn't simply remove it. You had to understand where the weight was going first, design a new path, build the frame that would receive it before you touched the wall at all. The opening became possible only once you understood where the load was going.

He picked up his pencil and drew the moment frame.

Priya, two years out of Cal Poly and still in the habit of arriving before him, appeared at his desk with a cup of tea and set it down without comment, then went back to her desk.

Oliver looked at the tea. He thought about Vicente's questions, the ones from Al-Anon he'd been practicing for fourteen months: *Did anyone ask you to? Are you the only one who can?* He had spent those months applying the questions to his behavior toward others, learning to pause before solving problems that hadn't been brought to him, learning to distinguish between help that was wanted and help that was a form of control dressed in generosity's clothing. He had not, until this moment, applied the questions to his behavior as the recipient.

Priya had offered care without being asked. He received it. No transaction had occurred. The tea was just tea, offered because she saw what was needed and had the capacity to provide it, and he accepted it because he needed it, and the whole exchange had taken thirty seconds and cost nothing and given him something he would not have given himself.

He thought about Callum. The three years of problems solved before they were problems, the future he built in his own mind and handed Callum to live inside of, as if the building had already been constructed and all Callum had to do was occupy it.

Priya didn't need to earn anything. She had simply seen and acted. She was just, without ceremony, being kind.

He understood then, holding the cup, that he had never once in three years allowed Callum to simply be kind to him without reciprocation, or a feeling of debt owed. Every act of care Callum offered, Oliver immediately exceeded—doubled, improved, preempted.

"Thank you," he said.

Priya nodded and went back to her desk. Oliver sipped the tea slowly while looking at the moment frame. He thought about structures built to receive a load and those that made the load necessary.

He finished the solution by three. Priya looked over his shoulder and confirmed: "That's it."

"That's it," he repeated.

She went back to her desk without ceremony. He sat for a moment longer looking at the final solution, at the frame that made the opening possible. His mind wandered back to what Paloma would find when she mapped him.

He thought: you can't simply remove the load-bearing wall cold turkey. You have to know where the weight will go first.

He put away his drawings and went to the Wednesday meeting.

The meeting was on the ground floor of a church on Dolores two blocks from his apartment, a grief-specific recovery group that met in a room smelling of old wood and candle wax. Ten or twelve people in folding chairs. The format was less liturgical than Al-Anon: people talked when they needed to, the silences were longer and less anxious, the room had a quality of being held rather than directed.

Oliver had been coming sporadically for four months, since Dr. Lim suggested it. He found it useful and uncomfortable, growth.

Tonight the share came from a man named Douglas who had lost his partner five years ago, not to a breakup but to death. He had been coming into this room ever since, with a regularity suggesting the room had become load-bearing for him. Douglas was a high school history teacher who spoke about grief the same way he taught history: with specificity. The details were where the meaning lived.

Tonight he talked about the problem of loving someone who could no longer receive it. He said the love didn't have anywhere to go. He said it kept arriving at an address that no longer existed and standing on the step with nowhere to put itself down. Even worse, if it's marked return to sender. He spent the first year going to all the places they frequented together: the taqueria on Mission, the bench in Dolores Park facing east, the movie theater in the Castro that still showed the films Marcus adored, conflating proximity to place with proximity to the person. He eventually understood he was conducting a séance with the city, returning to the locations hoping they would summon a semblance of Marcus, the feeling of him, the fact of him, back to him. It never did.

Instead, every time he went back to those places, he was honoring memories but in practice functioned like an open wound—keeping it from closing, keeping it fresh, pulling out the sutures.

Oliver sprawled uncomfortably over the folding chair that was far too small for his frame and felt the laser precision of a description that was not his yet called him out exactly.

The love that kept arriving at an address that no longer existed. He'd been standing on that stoop for three years. The difference was that Callum existed somewhere; he was alive, presumably, and moving through his own life. Technically locatable in principle even if not in practice. Which meant the address existed. Just not for Oliver. Not with a door that opened for him anymore.

He had thought, for most of the three years, that his situation was better than Douglas's. Not that it was healthy to make comparisons. He felt terrible thinking so, but at least Callum was alive. The future remained open for him. He understood then, for the first time, that he had been wrong. *A door wasn't just a hole in a wall to move through. It could instantly close and become a wall again. Especially with a lock from the other side.* For Oliver, a door that was simply closed produced its own harder grief. You could see the light peeking through underneath, hear the sounds on the other side, even stand on the other side every morning knowing the door could open, and yet did not. Also, Callum's *no* could be interpreted as a *not now*, not a *not ever.* Douglas's door was gone. Oliver's was right there.

He went back to what Dr. Osei had said: *the remnant learns your vulnerabilities well enough to use them.* He thought about his own East Bay pilgrimages: Willard Park, Dracena Quarry, Morcom Rose Garden. He had gone to all of them to burn sage in a ritual of cleansing. He believed he was releasing the memories held captive, performing a severance between place and person.

After the meeting, he stood by the coffee pot where Douglas found him, shorter than his voice suggested when seated, with a face creased into permanent vigilance. He poured a cup and handed it to Oliver without asking.

Oliver accepted it without commenting, more unwanted coffee.

"First time a share landed that way?" Douglas asked.

"I've heard versions of it before," Oliver replied, unsure what Douglas had picked up on. "Tonight hit differently."

Douglas nodded. "What changed?"

"I was diagnosed with a condition I've been wrestling with recently. Limbic residency, it can manifest as a more physical component called a remnant that can flare up in odd ways. It latches onto your own thought and feeling patterns, rituals, places you return to, even seeing people in others. I thought my East Bay trips were working through grief, but apparently I've just been feeding it agar material."

Douglas was quiet for a moment. "So you've been doing its bidding without knowing it."

"Apparently."

"Does that make the grief less real?"

Oliver had been sitting with this question since Dr. Osei's office. The grief was real. The love was real. The ring and the letters, they had felt entirely his, had come from what felt like the deepest part of him, even as the sage circuit kept expanding past any reasonable boundary. Just because the remnant had hijacked those expressions for its own purposes did not make the grief a fabrication. It made it an opportunistic infection exploiting genuine feeling to sustain itself.

"No," Oliver said. "It makes it more costly than I knew."

Douglas nodded slowly, looking down at his coffee. "The address," he said, referencing his own share. "That place you keep showing up at, where you keep returning to. You'll know when you stop going there to find him and start going to find yourself." He looked up. "Took me years to figure out when I switched from one to the other. Might take you less. You've got a name for what's happening to you. I just called it love."

Oliver held his look. "Wasn't it?"

"Sure it was." Douglas confirmed. "But it was also a story I was telling myself about me, and us. Both sides were true at the same time. That's what made it hard to let go." He finished his coffee. "The story felt the same as the love. Letting go of the story felt like letting go of the love for a long time."

He walked through the Mission afterward, further down Dolores, across the park where the fog sat low over the grass and the palms reached for the gray sky. He walked slowly, which was not his habit. He was a fast walker by nature, with a determined pace, destination always in mind. Tonight he let the street take longer than it needed, moving with the posture of a flaneur.

He passed one of the many panaderías on 24th closing up, the warm smell of conchas wafting through the entry as a customer carried trays inside. He passed a laundromat with a man outside watching his phone on autoplay. He passed the Ruth Bader Ginsburg bar with its door open and the sound of two people laughing freely. He passed back around, by the Mission Dolores, the old adobe church from 1776, low and thick-walled and still standing after all it's seen: the earthquakes, the fires, the missions themselves, two and a half centuries of the city building up and over and past it.

Oliver stopped outside, not from any religious impulse but from an architect's instinct toward buildings that outlasted their original context, sometimes for centuries.

He thought about Cassini.

He had been reading about the spacecraft for months, a tangent from his falling down a rabbit hole with Olbers, not research exactly, more like exploring a thread of inquiry that might yield unexpected results. NASA named its mission after another multitalented Giovanni who discovered four of Saturn's moons and observed the uneven division of its rings.

Mission Cassini launched in 1997, and traveled seven years through the solar system. To get to Saturn, though, it used gravity assists first from the opposite direction: Venus twice, then Earth, then Jupiter, each time borrowing the pull of a celestial body to go further than its own fuel could carry it. It arrived at Saturn in 2004 intact and ready, with enough fuel and instrumentation to begin the real mission: transmitting data no one had ever seen for thirteen years in orbit.

Standing in front of the steps of the Mission Dolores, Oliver thought about the gravity assist: real, significant, and necessary to the mission. It was the pull that had sent him further than he could have gone alone, though he had mistaken that assist for the arrival.

His mind wandered back to the remnant. The remnant had been organizing the same confusion through his limbic system, orienting toward Callum as destination, feeding on an already completed assist phase, without moving on. The gravity assist was over, yet it was still oriented toward a body whose pull it was no longer inside of.

Cassini's mission ended spectacularly after thirteen years in a Grand Finale. Mission scientists, knowing the fuel was nearly exhausted, made a deliberate choice: rather than let the spacecraft drift and potentially contaminate Saturn's moons, some of which could harbor conditions for life, they directed it into Saturn's atmosphere. Cassini threaded the gap between the planet and its innermost ring, a place no spacecraft had ever entered, twenty-two times, transmitting data until the signal went dark.

Oliver surfaced from the thought and came back onto the street in front of him. He remembered Paloma on Turk. His mind still wandered back into the parallels, diving into mission rather than drift. How to thread the gap between the planet and rings rather than orbit indefinitely at a safe distance. He took out his phone, and looked at the address again.

447 Turk.

He continued home.

At his dining table, he opened his letter document and looked over the pages for a long time. Then he wrote:

I've been reading about Cassini again. Seven years to Saturn. Four gravity assists. The spacecraft that traveled in the wrong direction first just to go further.

I confused the pull of your gravity for my destination. You weren't Saturn, but the assist was real. The arrival I imagined, though, was not.

Cassini's transmission went dark on September 15, 2017. It didn't drift. It flared up in a Grand Finale. I'm still transmitting. I don't know what I'm sending back data on, yet. Rings, moons, dust.

Proof someone went this far and found it worth recording. The light from other stars is no mystery. The mystery is what stops it from passing through.

P.S. Remember, I have loved you.

He closed the laptop. He looked at the ring on his left hand.

He left it where it was.

Chapter Three: Structural Release

447 Turk was an Edwardian painted the color of old bone, peeling, narrow between two buildings that had been there longer. The Tenderloin on a Thursday afternoon: a man sleeping on the steps next door; the smell of rice scorched from the Vietnamese restaurant across the street; a woman in a gold headscarf speaking into her phone in a language Oliver couldn't place. He stood at the base of the steps and looked at the door, which was painted dark green like the utility poles Department of Public Works repaints many times over and held traces of its earlier shades in the cracks.

He checked the address again: 447. This was it.

There was no buzzer. He knocked.

He had left work early, clearing his afternoon in the calendar with a block labeled drawing review and hoped Priya could cover without comment. He dropped off his messenger bag and took a few minutes to empty his head. The route from his apartment took thirty minutes and consisted of a route through several neighborhoods with no official border from one to the other: the Mission, Hayes Valley, Civic Center, and the Tenderloin, which was its own autonomous territory for as long as Oliver could remember. He walked because his body in movement did what staring at drawings couldn't—let the solution arrive on its own. He had learned to make that distinction in therapy.

The door opened.

The woman who answered was shorter than he expected from a name like Paloma and what Vicente had offered, which was nothing. She wore reading glasses pushed up into her dark gray hair, and a canvas apron over a linen shirt. Her face had been arranged by a succession of difficult conversations over decades into one that no longer needed to perform composure; it had solidified into composure at rest. Oliver estimated she was somewhere past late fifties. After a certain threshold, age flattened into approximation.

"Oliver," she said. It was not a question.

"Yes."

She stepped back and let him in.

The interior didn't announce itself. A space arranged by someone who understood what a room said before anyone looked at it directly. Low ceilings adapted from the parlor floor into an area that wasn't quite a waiting room yet also wasn't quite a salon. Two chairs upholstered in faded blue wool, pilling. A table with tea and three ceramic cups. Bookshelves along the north wall, floor-to-ceiling, spines creased from use and interspersed with objects whose function was not immediately obvious at a glance: a glass orb, a carved wooden bird, a length of braided cord. Two dim floor lamps with the sunlight coming through the west window's drapes, the rich gold preceding the velvet navy of dusk, lasting exactly long enough to notice before the switch flipped instantly.

A man Oliver didn't recognize sat in the second chair.

Oliver's approximate age, heavier in the shoulders, with paint along the base of his right thumb he either hadn't noticed or had ceased to care about. He looked up when Oliver came in, looking him over with the forced, disciplined patience of someone who gave up on expecting time to move faster.

"Santi," he said, remaining seated, but raising his hand.

"Oliver."

Paloma had gone through a door in the back and did not reappear immediately. Oliver stayed standing for a moment, then sat in the open chair. Santi looked at him, then back at the bookshelves. A minute passed avoiding eye contact.

"First time?" Santi said.

"Yes."

"Mapping or excision?"

"Mapping. First session."

Santi nodded. "You know about the three session minimum? Two mapping, one excision. She told you?"

"Vicente told me."

A change crossed Santi's expression. "Vicente sent you?"

"You know him?"

"No. But Paloma mentioned him. Before everything had a product name." He looked at Oliver's left hand. "Stage III?"

Oliver looked at his own hand, the ring, as if seeing it from outside himself. "Yes."

"I was Stage II when I came in. She said I could've managed with suppression, but I decided I didn't want to manage." Santi started looking over the bookshelves. "I left, but the remnant doesn't understand the difference between leaving because I had to, leaving because I wanted to, and leaving because I was wrong. It just encoded the separation."

Oliver listened.

"Her name is Linea," Santi said. "I left her to come here. From Amsterdam." He paused. "But the remnant didn't see it that way, *doesn't* see it that way." He stopped, as if catching himself oversharing. "Anyway. Paloma doesn't rush. Let it take the time it takes."

Paloma's workroom was at the back of the house, past the kitchen, through a door widened from its original frame past Edwardian proportions. Long and low-lit, with north-facing windows that gave the even gray light the master Dutch painters in Delft looked for. A padded table at the center, positioned lengthwise rather than against a wall. A desk to the left with a scanner Oliver recognized as a consumer variant of the clinic model, same manufacturer, different generation, just one or two behind.

A second, smaller device sat beside it: with sensor leads arrayed like a crown of wires, calibrated to a frequency the display wasn't built to show.

"Sit," Paloma said, indicating the table's edge. She was still wearing the apron. She didn't make a ceremony out of the purely functional room.

Oliver sat. He looked at the scanner.

"We're not starting with that," she said. "Vicente told me your results. I've seen the scan. I know what Dr. Osei showed you." She sat at the desk, turned toward him. "I need to know what she didn't show you. What it was like before the diagnosis. What it's been like since. The whole history. Not the clinical summary. The version you've been carrying."

"Where do I start?"

"Where it hurts most."

This was the opposite of therapy. Dr. Lim asked questions that circled, that let him arrive on his own terms. This was a direct request, transactional even. He thought about it for a long moment, not how to begin but which beginning was true.

"I wrote to him last night," he said. "Like I do nearly every night for the past three years. The letters are in a running document I never share. It's the only place I'm entirely honest about what I'm going through."

Paloma said nothing. Which to him meant: continue.

"Last night I wrote about NASA's Mission Cassini, the spacecraft.

I've been reading about it on and off for months, circling back to it. The gravity assists, the thirteen years in orbit, the flaring up at the end." He paused. "I wrote that I confused his gravity for my destination."

"Who is he?"

"Callum."

"What did he do?"

Oliver thought about how to answer in the truest way. "I proposed; he said no. But in a genuinely kind way that continues to eat at me. And then he left." He looked at the floor. "He said he needed to work through his social trauma on his own. That he couldn't do it in a relationship. That he might not be cut out for one." He wasn't sure he should continue. Paloma looked at him in silence. "He was right to. For his own part—and mine. The Al-Anon work with Vicente made that clear. I was building a future for us in my mind and handing it to him to live out. I wrote a version of this as an amends in the letter doc." He stopped. "But I don't think the remnant knows any of that. It's just looping three years of him encoded in my mind."

"The prosopagnosia," Paloma said. "The clinic told you about the false matches."

"Dr. Osei called them feeding events."

Paloma nodded slowly, though not in agreement, more in the manner of acknowledging what a younger generation calls the same phenomenon. "The clinic's language is accurate as far as that goes," she said. "The remnant uses the prosopagnosia as metabolic infrastructure. Every false match gives it what it needs, that's true." She looked at him directly. "What the clinic didn't tell you is that the feeding isn't what the remnant does to you, but through you. It found your preexisting prosopagnosia and learned to harness it. Your brain automatically scans for pattern matches as a workaround for identifying people. The remnant hijacked the workaround and made sure Callum's pattern kept coming." A pause. "Every false match triggers the same emotional response as actually seeing him would. That's what it runs on."

Oliver absorbed the new information on the remnant. "That doesn't make me feel better."

"It's not meant to." She stood and moved toward the scanner. "I'm going to survey your limbic system for a baseline map, more comprehensive than what the clinic did. They only look for what they can measure according to their parameters. I'm looking for the whole picture, how the remnant organized itself around your existing patterns, not just where it lodged."

"Is there a difference?"

"Yes, significantly." She picked up the crown of wires and held it. "The clinic sees the consolidation. The mass, the stage. What they can't classify is the behavioral dynamic: how the remnant learned to use your own rituals, your own language, your own worldview against you." She looked at him. "Vicente mentioned you're in Al-Anon."

"On and off, but fourteen months with him as my sponsor."

"And before the diagnosis, the Stepwork, was that working?"

"Yes and no. I was doing the work. The codependency patterns were becoming clear. I learned a lot." He stopped. "But then I realized the East Bay pilgrimages weren't grieving. They were feeding events dressed up as healing. The remnant was steering the rituals."

"What was the ratio," Paloma said. "In the rituals. What part was yours?"

This was the question he kept himself from arriving at since Dr. Osei's office. He thought along the edges, the way he thought around Callum in the mornings—running his hand along the brick perimeter wall.

"I don't know," he said. That was all he had.

"That's consistent with Stage III. The dissolution of the border between your grief and the remnant." She came toward him with the crown of wires. "Lean back. Just stay present and breathe. If something surfaces, let it. Don't try to manage it or avoid it."

Oliver lay back on the table. He looked at the ceiling, plaster, original, with the hairline cracks of surviving 1906 and 1989 and the in-between by redistributing strain in ways newer construction didn't.

The crown felt heavy on his head. It didn't feel like the sleek clinic scanner. There he had watched the process on a screen, the image of his own limbic system visible as bone in an x-ray. This was different. The leads made contact at the temples and the base of the skull and somewhere above and behind the ears. Nothing registered in a way he could have named as sensation. But the room changed texture, like when a constant background sound you hadn't consciously noticed stopped all of a sudden.

The remnant on mute, he thought.

"Tell me about the ring," Paloma said. She was at the desk. He couldn't see her from his periphery. Her voice arrived as a prompt, part of an interrogation, not asking in order to make polite conversation.

"He loved trees. I bought it in Mill Valley. I was waiting for a friend. It's made of salvaged koa wood. Two whale tails carved that meet but don't enclose." A pause. "He also loved whales."

"When did you decide to buy it."

"I was in the shop for about fifteen minutes. Part of me knew as soon as I saw it, though I continued to browse." He stopped again mulling on whether to continue. "I was holding onto the possibility of proposing to him again. That this time his answer would be different."

He couldn't see her, but Oliver swore he could feel Paloma's face change, as if she realized this was going to be harder than she first imagined when agreeing to take him on from Vicente.

Oliver went back to Vicente's question, did anyone ask you to?, and the version of that question that applied here. "I've asked myself since whether the decision was mine."

"What do you think?" She was entering Dr. Lim territory, and for a split second, Oliver wondered if this was a trick question.

"It certainly felt like mine, but also not entirely conscious and explicit, like when you have a thought or feeling but don't have the words. It felt like the purest expression of knowing him." He stopped. "Maybe the remnant had been reading me for months before I walked into the shop. It recognized the ring the same way it recognizes the false faces around town before I do. Before my conscious mind arrives."

Silence. Not an expectant kind, the silence of preoccupied concentration and calibration.

"The first time you saw someone you thought was him," Paloma said. "Before the limbic residency diagnosis."

Oliver thought back. "It was on a BART platform, a few months after Callum left. My chest compressed and then I went through my verification checklist: wrong shoes, wrong gait, wrong everything except the outline." A pause. "I thought my brain was playing tricks on me from the loss. I thought: this is what missing him looks like when I'm out in the world, not just in my head at home. A soul that keeps looking for the person who's gone."

"And just to confirm, you already had prosopagnosia? Before

Callum," Paloma said. "So the remnant didn't create this mechanism. The distinction matters for the exorcism. If the remnant spawned it on its own, the exorcism is cleaner. If it learned to use what was already yours—" She didn't finish. He understood: the extraction would require deeper digging and more precision.

"The writing," Paloma prompted, moving on in a hard pivot. "The letters."

"My therapist, Dr. Lim suggested it as a bounded practice. Write it down, don't send it. It started out just once in a while when I felt like I needed to talk to him. Then it became more like journaling, sometimes a casual one sided conversation, and more frequent over the years." He stopped again wondering whether to continue. "And after the first year or two, it was where I could speak without worrying what anyone else thought, without risking my friends getting sick of hearing me talk about it."

"What did you write about last night?"

He already told her about Cassini. But she was asking for specifics. "I wrote about Cassini's Grand Finale. How mission scientists made a deliberate choice rather than let the spacecraft drift to the unknown. They directed it into the atmosphere to burn up rather than let it contaminate the moons that might harbor future life." He stared at the ceiling." I wrote: I'm still transmitting. I don't know yet what I'm sending back data on."

The room was quiet for a long time. Oliver started getting antsy lying there still.

"What do you want," Paloma said. A flat statement.

Oliver wondered if she worked from a script. It would explain the pacing.

The question arrived without context and without any priming to invite a sanitized answer. He lay on the table with the crown of wires and for the first time in three years, thought directly about what he wanted.

"I want to know which parts of the last three years were mine," he said. "I want to know how to move on if the remnant weren't running its own agenda through me." He paused. "I want to see someone on the street, have no thoughts or recognition, and keep walking."

"What else."

Wanting more felt like a luxury. He racked his brain. He was the student who needed to answer if the classroom stayed quiet longer than a minute after a teacher's question. There he was again, quiet for longer than felt comfortable.

"I want to stop waking up." He paused before adding, "So early," grinning to himself.

—

The mapping took an hour and twenty minutes. Oliver learned this afterward; he had no reliable sense of the time while it was happening, similar to when he was getting tattooed, without the overt physical pain and grimacing. What he could report was that at some point his consciousness drifted, not into sleep per se, nor the limbo towards it, but he recognized he was failing his one task to remain present. The sound of the tattoo gun and the feeling of the inked needle on his skin sent him, like certain songs, to a bardo, similar to where he found himself now. He was aware of the room but also the bardo place that was not the room. He thought of himself as a building that knew of its foundation: not consciously, but in every load-bearing way, the whole existence depending on what was underneath.

He found himself again in one of Piranesi's prisons. The elaborate torture contraptions, the arches on arches, the implied purpose without provision. He had been almost right, looking at the Stage III scan. The remnant wasn't the prison; that was his mind. The remnant was the damp that gets into old stone and works its way through the joins, until a mason can no longer differentiate cleanly: this is original, this is damage.

He thought about Callum, the keystone in the central archway of his prison.

He thought about him directly: the specific quality of his attention when he listened, which was total in a way Oliver had never felt from anyone before or since despite spending three years trying to find again. The way he identified trees by their bark rather than their leaves, running one hand along the trunk with intentional patience, understanding that some information arrives on its own time. Anam ċara: a presence making you feel more fully yourself.

I wasn't wrong to love him, he thought. *I was wrong about what loving him required of me.*

The realization arrived without argument, delivered through a side door left ajar. For once, he let it arrive without trying to defend against it. It arrived in a way Oliver could finally receive.

When Paloma removed the wires, his neck was stiff and the light through the windows had gone blue. Dusk. He hated when that happened, like when he entered a movie theater while still light out and afterward, came out into the dark.

Paloma sat at the desk looking at the readout on the secondary display, which showed a mix of lines, dots, and abstract shapes Oliver couldn't interpret from where he sat. Rasterized densities and vectors, perhaps. The isometric drawing showing how the building came together rather than the photograph of the direct facade.

"You can sit up," she said, without looking away from the display.

He sat up slowly. He felt wrung out, like after certain sessions with Dr. Lim where an insight was reached rather than orbited for the entire fifty minutes. It was a productive exhaustion that Oliver felt proud of and hopeful from.

"What did you find?" he asked.

"What I expected based on the scans from the clinic, and one surprise." She turned to look at him. "The remnant is organized exactly the way Stage III presents. The limbic consolidation, the prefrontal threading, the sleep-cycle integration. Dr. Osei's read is accurate." A pause. "What I didn't expect is how organized it is around absence rather than memory."

Oliver looked at her.

"Most Stage III remnants organize around the encoded data," Paloma said. "Retinal images, voice, the sensory record of the other person. They consolidate around what was there." She looked at the display. "Yours organized around the shape of what wasn't. The gap." She let this sink in. "Callum's absence is the organizing architecture. The memories are furniture. But the remnant isn't living in your memories of him; it's living in the negative space, the outline of him. The space where he would've been."

Oliver flashed back to his readings of Olbers. If the universe is infinite and full of stars, the night sky should be blazing.

"Olbers' paradox," he murmured.

Paloma looked at him with an expression signalling not quite surprise but adjacent, a blend of intrigued amusement, wanting to hear how a patient arrived with their own language and understanding.

"Explain," she stated.

"The remnant organized around the darkness, not the light," he said.

"I've been treating his absence as distance, light that hasn't arrived yet. Still coming. The remnant found that belief and built itself inside it."

"And the light that hasn't arrived—"

"Might never," Oliver said. "And yet the darkness isn't emptiness. It's still full of what's moving toward it, or at least, what could be moving toward it. I guess there's no guarantee."

Paloma wrote a few lines in silence.

"It isn't conscious," Paloma started. "I want to be clear about that. It doesn't want you to suffer and it doesn't want you to heal. It doesn't want anything. It persists through whatever conditions allow itself to persist, like any nonsentient organism does, well, maybe the most similar comparison is to a virus. It found your grief already there, already substantial, and learned to live inside it. It recognized your behavior as conditions favorable to its survival and steered them toward continuation. You were always going to love him. The remnant just knew how to make the loving keep it alive."

She turned back to the display. "What's yours is the grief. The love. The coping strategies you've built to carry the experience: Olbers, Piranesi, the letters." She looked at him over the monitors. "The remnant claimed the hole itself. Not absence—density. Not nothingness—possibility. A hole and a void aren't the same. The remnant knew that before you did. It moved into the gravitational center of the hole and made a resonant field there. Anything that kept the hole open rather than allowing it to close."

Oliver sat with this for a long moment.

"The morning checks," he said.

"Early grief produces those kinds of checking patterns naturally. It's the psyche's way of assessing damage and processing after trauma, another form of encoding. The remnant recognized the behavior and appropriated it. By now it's been running them long enough that the distinction has collapsed." She folded her hands. "The exorcism won't feel like losing the grief. The grief is still yours. It'll feel lighter, though, as if you've been carrying an outsize weight because it hitched a ride at the same time."

Oliver thought about his molar, and the oral surgeon saying he was surprised Oliver came in without screaming in agony. The infection had killed the nerve endings. It had made itself comfortable where he couldn't feel it.

"When's the second session?" he asked.

"Next week. Same time." She looked at him. "I want you to write to him tonight, knowing what you know now, that the gap is the remnant's and the love is yours." She paused. Oliver wasn't sure this was great advice for moving on, but he was willing to trust the process. "Also, tomorrow morning, see what's left when you take the checks away."

He let himself out, past the entry room where Santi's chair was empty now, the ceramic cups washed and stacked, the water pitcher refilled and waiting. The door onto Turk opened into a late Thursday evening: the woman in the gold headscarf was now seated on the steps two buildings over, phone in her lap; a child on a skateboard navigating the sidewalk with hypervigilant focus to avoid catching his wheels in the debris scattered across, as if the entire sidewalk were the childhood classic *floor is lava*.

Oliver stood for a moment on the stoop of the steps.

The fog was fully in. The city softened, edges gone, sounds muffled from no clear direction. He could still smell the aromas drifting from the Vietnamese restaurant and, underneath it, the mineral scent of fog misting the concrete. It was a nostalgic smell he associated with San Francisco itself: cold dampness settling into asphalt, brick, metal railings, the mix recognizable as home. The only other times he encountered anything close was after a heavy summer rain elsewhere, when the heat rose back out of wet pavement as the streets dried and the evaporation threw a similar mineral scent into the air.

He thought about Santi in the waiting room. The remnant of Linea that had appeared even though he was the one to leave her, rather than the other way around. Perhaps the remnant didn't recognize directionality, only the end effect.

His own remnant had encoded the *no*, a two-letter reply delivered with gentle kindness by a man who had to walk through his own valley, alone. The remnant didn't know anything about the context. As Paloma said, it didn't care; it didn't want. The remnant had just encoded: this gravitational force was here, and then he wasn't.

Oliver started putting one foot in front of the other to generate enough inertia to carry him home and clear his mind. He walked slowly, ambulating, as if recovering after a procedure, which was technically the case, regardless of what any medical establishment might say.

Waiting for the light to cross at Hyde, he took out his phone. He opened the document. Three years of letters, running in continuous unsent sequence, the record of a diary or a confession box in a Catholic cathedral, a quiet place to be entirely honest while presenting a different face to the noisy outside world.

He started typing:

I went to Turk St to see Paloma. She put a crown of wires on my head and mapped what you left behind, the aftermath. She said the remnant organized itself around your absence rather than your presence. Not the memories, but the shape of where you would have been.

He put his phone back in his pocket, and looked up at the sky. It had turned dark orange from the hazy fog lit and crowned with halos by the streetlights underneath, from a city that didn't go dark, and contained no visible stars.

He kept going through it anyway.

II. Essays

⌜*Fata obstant.* Fate stands in the way (4.440). But Dido can't understand that. She does not have the means of understanding it. She has not just been abandoned by Aeneas; as we have already said, she has abandoned herself. Dido is even deaf to the hero's one true declaration of love. Virgil writes that, yes, Aeneas is resolved to leave, but he is still *magnoque animum labefactus*: shaken in his soul by his great love for her (4.395). ⌟

Marcolongo, *Starting from Scratch*

We always knew we'd be lovers
When the summer ends
Can't stand to be apart from one another
On the other hand
We weren't fit to play
Like kings and queens before
And now I'm sleeping with the lights on looking over my shoulder
And double bolting the door

How Sad, *Hot Blur*

Frames of Reference

I heard from multiple sources that Vassar was a *very* gay *performing arts school*. I had never done anything performing arts related in my life—unless performing heteronormativity counted, in which case I had my then entire life's worth. What I told my parents was that I wanted a liberal arts education. My mother, from her own background as an electrical engineer and first generation immigrant from China, only knew of universities and their engineering schools. She was very concerned, if not only because this unfamiliar college was described solely by the words *liberal* and *arts*. We were locked in a long, drawn out negotiation that we still no longer talk about to this day. I never *came out* because when I left the midwest, I left that closeted boy as well—it wasn't so much reinvention as reintroduction, with salient features that no one else had previously cared about.

The director Nathan Baumbach went to Vassar too, a few decades before he became known for filming arrested adulthoods. He shot *Frances Ha* (2012) in the same student union I passed everyday, while I was still there even. I saw Meryl Streep on campus on top of a pickup bed in an inconspicuous outfit of sunglasses, baseball cap, and oversized chore jacket, helping her daughter move in or out. I mingled at the Aula within 10ft of Lisa Kudrow, but didn't want to be *that* student fan. I didn't care much for celebrity at the time, and even now, I'd rather have a short chat, a personalized note, or an author's signature in my well worn book.

From what I could tell, Vassar knew how to produce stars who were talented *and* smart. I didn't understand most of the theater I saw, experimental or canon, nor did I ever stop believing that the Drama-102 finals were just a ruse to exhibit nudity in more and more outlandish fashion. During my time there, Kudrow delivered the 2011 commencement address, sharing how she majored in neuroscience and conducted research on headaches before becoming the actress many of us remember as Phoebe from *Friends*. I laughed when she declared, *I won't bore you with the details of headaches, but I could!*, as my first boyfriend graduated years ahead of me. I insist *Frances Ha* isn't a romance, but it behaves like one: two women read a single friendship in two incompatible ways, each certain her version is the accurate vision.

I went into my second try at a freshman year hoping to experience a romantic relationship, one I'd been longing for since becoming an adolescent in Indiana and then boarding school after. By then, I'd seen *500 Days of Summer* and cherished its portrayal, even as the hipsters surrounding me eviscerated it from their reflexive refusal to feel anything so baldly and sincerely. I still hold sincerity and authenticity dearly. In a pivotal scene revealed only after several time jumps across the span of their relationship, Tom and Summer sit casually at a diner booth when the floor drops underneath one of them. The film directly references a series of classics, so to me, this particular setting recalls *When Harry Met Sally* (1989), and even the start of *Pulp Fiction* (1994), given the Sid and Nancy reference. Summer reveals the breakup shouldn't come as a surprise to Tom: they've been like Sid and Nancy for months. Tom corrects her hyperbole: Sid stabbed Nancy seven times with a kitchen knife. A few disagreements didn't make him homicidal. *No...I'm Sid,* she explains. Then, a stunned Tom, *So I'm Nancy*‽

Two lovers can participate in the same relationship, each holding a different version, sometimes involving a knife. In modern physics, superposition allows for two contradictory states to exist at once, both true, until measurement collapses the observation into a single outcome, a forcing function. Tom and Summer never agree on which of them was Sid and which was Nancy, not that the relationship nor the breakup hinged on the exact role. Lived life is often more like that quantum superposition: sometimes, we're Sid, and sometimes, we're Nancy. Often, we don't know which until we're confronted with a situation to measure ourselves against. Until the diner booth forced Tom and Summer to share their perspectives out loud, each could believe they were one or the other. Tom walks out, and Summer yells after him, in a slowed reverb, *Tom, don't. Come back. You're still my best fri—end.* Conor and I decided to go no contact for the past couple of years, so I don't even get a best friend out of our relationship.

While we had differences in our personal philosophies, we aligned on the core foundations. I still hope he'll be in my life in one way or another down the line. As I've been excavating our relationship and comparing it against those in film and literature, I realized that like Tom and Summer, we were occupying two parallel tracks, both true, yet separate, lacking an elegant way to join them together how I wanted, like a double helix in DNA.

Conor once shared that our relationship reminded him of Connell and Marianne in *Normal People* by Sally Rooney. We were on the couch, half-watching a movie we never ended up finishing. He said it offhandedly, low stakes, already halfway onto the next sentence. Perhaps he missed the loadbearing weight of what he was saying, or maybe he was too scared to dwell on it. With me, he didn't perform. He didn't mentally check his face for the appropriate expression before letting it settle. He said he felt comfortable, safe. We created our world together, and I was more than happy to stay in it. He had spent high school eating lunch alone in the library rather than risking the cafeteria. I had spent every day of the academic year with the same five boys wondering why we never ate meals when *I* wanted. Some days he locked himself in a bathroom stall until the period bell rang, waiting out his peers from afar. Some days, I disappeared into the East Gym, to lose myself by myself. He shared those stories with me as a matter of fact, the way he might describe the weather when we packed for travel. I never shared these stories with him, with anyone.

I took his comparison to *Normal People* as romantic, and a testament to our relationship. I didn't ask which half of the pair he thought was me and which was him, since again, the exact role didn't matter. I eventually learned he meant I was his Connell: steady, unbothered, the one whose regard could quiet a room in his head. Someone he could feel completely himself around. I've always felt more like Marianne: the one who needs someone else's certainty to put on, who runs anxious under a competent facade, who doesn't feel as steady on the inside as I apparently seemed to him from his side of the couch. While he wasn't performing for me, I don't know that I ever stopped performing for anyone, including myself. It was only in the aftermath that I revealed the true nature of myself—to myself.

What does it mean for two people to each be the other's Connell? He said I was his, and I was too flustered at the time to let it sink in. He was always mine, that was a given for me: the one person around whom I let my guard down, who could steady the eye of my hurricane, who brought out a more loving version of me, in our world and out. Both of us held the other, neither of us saying so with words.

Near the end, he compared us again, this time to Aksel and Julie from *The Worst Person in the World* (2021). He shared it on the long, slow way to our breaking up, in a tone that conveyed he'd been thinking about the comparison since first seeing the film. He was envious, he told me, of how sure I was that he was the one, Aksel-sure. He had never managed that: not about me, and, he suspected, not about anyone, given his own constitution and fear. He wondered aloud whether he was built for a romantic relationship at all, or whether he'd end up in a monastery far away, robed and settled. Julie-unsure, except Julie eventually chooses, or rather, life chooses for her. Conor wasn't even promising me that.

Tom and Summer never agree on who held the knife, though the breakup stems from Summer. Conor and I didn't agree near the end, but what could I say? He said he felt too comfortable with me; he wasn't pushing himself to grow socially and meet new friends because it was always easier to default to being with me. Two people describing a same slow motion collapse from different distances, at different velocities will see it differently from each position, but neither is wrong.

In an essay I return to by Natalia Ginzburg, *He and I,* she describes her marriage in matching, opposite halves: his habits set against hers, his certainties against her doubts, until the two portraits no longer resemble either one singularly from the outside. At the closing, she recalls a walk the two of them took early on, shortly after they met and before the rest of their relationship developed. They were strolling on the Via Nazionale in Rome against the setting sun. She says if she brings up that walk now, decades later, he'll say he remembers it, too. But she doesn't believe him. She suspects the walk only survives in her memory—that if anything, he simply pictures two acquaintances trading pleasantries, courteous strangers who could've said goodbye forever at the corner without any remorse for what could have been.

Conor and I had our own version of this walk during our first fall together. It was during the Midautumn Moon festival, when I shared mooncakes with his parents, and then the two of us went off on our own, like most nights during the pandemic. This night, we went down a path under fairy lights along a bridge near his family home. The moon was bright, but the clouds were hazy, casting a haloed crown. I doubt that night meant the same for him as it did for me, not because I don't believe he remembers it, but because I no longer trust we remember the same tenor of that night, or any other point in our relationship together. He recalls a boy who felt, for the first time, unwatched. I recall that same boy calling me his rock, while I stood to smile, and didn't correct him.

Frances Ha doesn't end in a couple, romantic or otherwise, despite

Frances navigating others' relationships. After a stretch of subletting other people's lives and apartments, Frances gets her own. She writes her full name, Frances Halladay, on a slip of paper too long for the mailbox label and folds it over to fit. I used to view this scene as diminishment, shrinking to fit within a prescribed frame. Now I view it as Frances assuming full agency in her own way. The frame was never too small nor the paper too long. She could've used any other permutation of her name: just her first, her last, her initials, or even narrower script, tighter kerning. She quickly and playfully decides who and what fits, and how.

Conor called me Connell, folding me in, calling me by his name. I've never stopped feeling like Marianne. Both are true, superpositioned, with no measurement forcing either one into direct observation. He was my Connell, too. Neither of us has to be wrong for the other to be right.

God, that was strange to see you again
Introduced by a friend of a friend
Smiled and said, "Yes, I think we've met before"
In that instant, it started to pour
....
Live through this and you won't look back

Stars, *Your Ex-Lover Is Dead*

Frequency Illusions

It was the quality of light, on that early clear morning, in the bakery's garden that sent me back to a similarly familiar morning, years ago, when I first took Conor there. I was even wearing the same shirt as that day—memorialized in a photo we took when we seemed like two different people, not us, not so long ago.

Frequency illusion refers to a cognitive bias where a person starts noticing a specific word or concept more frequently after learning about it. The first recorded example for the phenomenon occurred with the name of the Baader–Meinhof terrorist group, where once a reader learned of it, he kept noticing it. Scientists suspect the illusion occurs from an interaction of two psychological processes: selective attention and confirmation bias.

After the bakery, and the rest of our Sebastopol ritual, including the coffee shop Retrograde and the spiritual bookstore Many Rivers next door, my close friend Adrián wanted to stop at a new lunch spot in Mill Valley on our way back. On the short walk downtown, we passed a restaurant patio that gave me déjà vu. It only took a long second to remember the rainy evening dinner where we celebrated our first anniversary.

When we turned the corner, Adrián wanted to see the inside of a Catholic church across the way. I was too hot and tired by then, so I stayed along the shaded bend and ducked inside a little shop. It was filled with *objets d'arts* from artisans around the world. The curation contained a strong sense of *Marin New Age for the Modern Woman*, including a deck of oracle-adjacent cards titled *I Married Myself*. I rolled my eyes despite living in a way that could be described as such after I proposed to Conor—and he counterproposed parting ways. Not what I had in mind when I asked him to marry me, but that was the hand I was dealt from a different kind of oracle-adjacent deck.

As I continued scoffing to myself through the rest of the shop until Adrián finished, I saw it: a bronze ring with two whale tails that met but didn't fully enclose: a similar theme as the salvaged koa one I'd proposed to Conor with. He loved trees first but also whales. *Selective attention*: I miss him, so I see him everywhere.

I bought the ring and wondered if I could use it one day to propose to him again. The next week, I met a man named Chance at a Polaroid photography conference. As we exchanged numbers via Apple's *Name Drop* feature, I saw his very Dutch surname and very un-American suffix—II—as in the second, rather than junior. He joked with a prepared line: he was *a second chance*. He couldn't know how hard the metaphor hit. Here he was grinning at me, and all I could manage was a fake smile back, privately wishing for Conor. The weekend after, I came across a poem about chance encounters and shared it with him despite never getting close enough to ask, *will there be a third*?

I wore the whale tails on my own ring finger in an attempt at solace for the time being. Three days later, I lost it—or rather, it fell off on its own, and I started turning into Gollum from *The Lord of the Rings* with a similar obsessive desperation for his *precious*. I was walking out early in the morning for a 7 am fellowship and turned the corner when it hit me: I didn't feel it on my hand. I considered continuing and looking for it when I came back, but I knew my mind would obsess. I turned around and scoured the path back inside, up the patterned carpet stairs, and inch by inch on my knees on the wood floors of my apartment. I texted my neighbors to look out for it. I needed eyes to cover the less than forty feet total outside of my own apartment. I shined a flashlight hoping the bronze would glint back and catch my eye. After the third pass, I looked up to see if bronze was magnetic, thinking I could use a giant magnet or metal detector—anything to bring it back to me.

I processed the stages of grief in rapid succession. At 7 am I bargained. Then I yelled, expletives included. My roommate was away, thankfully, but I also considered opening a window for a proper primal scream to the world. I refused to read into the metaphor of the situation despite the reality pressing in on me. My mind was melting down. I could see it happening at an inner remove, what I imagine the colloquial phrase *watching a slow motion train wreck* refers to, except it's just me with my own mind. When it's happened before, I never knew how it would end. Would my mind crumple like sheet metal crushed by an SUV? Or pop back like a bumper in a low-speed fender bender? I've fallen into depressions for far less, sometimes for no apparent reason at all. By the end of the hour at 8 am, I had come back out of the sunken depths: a personal record. It was a humbling masterclass for acceptance and detachment, condensed into an hour. In the aftermath, I still griped about the loss to those who would understand. Every now and then, anxiety would still tug, and I'd scan the floors again. Surely I'd find it this time. Instead, the kitchen linoleum asked desperately for mopping.

Four days after the loss, I caught up with an absent acquaintance and former friend, Taylor, whose boyfriend had proposed in the long gap between our last meeting. When I saw Taylor's engagement ring, I had to laugh. It was the same ring I used to propose to Conor, made from salvaged koa from Hawaii. Like me, Taylor was *quapa*, a portmanteau of a quarter hapa, albeit reversed with a Japanese grandpa who grew up in Hawaii. Perhaps that's more connection to koa relative to Conor's and my quarter Irish love of trees, but I couldn't find any rings made from salvaged ash or elm. I felt smug for knowing the lore behind the ring, but was I supposed to feel happy for Taylor? I was much too mired in my own mess to feel anything for him at all. Besides, most of my headspace was preoccupied resenting God for winking at me with His sense of humor.

Three days afterward, I found the whale tail ring. It had fallen off in the tote bag I was preparing that morning. When I grabbed it again, I felt the tails' pointy edges and knew. A deluge of relief washed over me. And then, just as quickly, the dilemma of whether I would ever wear it out again appeared. My mind wandered into metaphor again. Do I keep the ring safe at home, never to risk losing again? Or do I wear it out in remembrance? I chose to wear it. I already processed the loss and grief once. I could survive it again.

If I were to wallow in metaphor, I should be hearing from Conor any day now, like a Shakespearean play within a play. Here's a timeline of upcoming chances: his spring break, our anniversary, his birthday, summer break. Nothing I do can manifest hearing from him, despite my many petitions. Therapy alone isn't doing it. Neither is the prayer. I needed more firepower.

As a self-appointed doula for moving past this threshold, I concocted new rituals including bringing garden sage with me to burn whenever I'm in Berkeley or Oakland. When I pass a place haunted with memories: his old church on College he insisted on taking me to, the bakery on Adeline whose ostentatious confetti cake we loved for celebrating, another church on Telegraph where he attended AA meetings. *Confirmation bias*: these hauntings pop-up everywhere.

After a few of these unplanned sightings, I took control and deliberately sought out the monumental sites. I wanted to confront them, these places that made me incapable of looking on without a shudder of simultaneous fond memory and profound loss. Armed with the sage and a cheap matchbook, I hoped direct confrontation would hasten the process: Willard Park, where we shared our first in-person picnic date during the pandemic; Dracena Quarry, the endpoint of a walk we liked after dinner with his parents at his family home; Morcom Rose Garden, where he showed me the spots he went to clear his head, appreciate beauty, find gratitude.

Smoke censing for purification has a long lineage from ancient Egypt and Rome with frankincense and myrrh to the Celtic islands with juniper saining to East Asia with incense for Buddhist meditation. Closer to home, the Indigenous North American nations view white sage as sacred medicine also used to purify. In my declassé ritual, the common garden sage smokes the memories out, like the modern equivalent of an outdoor juice cleanse.

The entire Bay Area, and then some, is haunted. Forestville, where he grew up spending the summers at an uncle's, the hidden entry point along the Russian River where he showed me how to tube without the crowds, the riverbend where I first told him I loved him. Nearby Guerneville, where I enjoyed the pie and ice cream, and he preferred the biscuits. Sea Ranch, where I took him with my family over the winter holidays—a stretch of foggy Mendocino coast where I knew he must have really loved me to endure my family in a cabin for a week. In the opposite direction, Monterey, where we had one of our first overnight trips. Big Sur, where a hermitage lies atop the cliffs, overlooking the ocean, and where I go in retreat, where I invited him in, further still. San Luis Obispo, where I brought him to meet my godmother—the only partner I've ever introduced to her—for whatever reason more momentous than introducing him to my own.

I'm not sure I can exorcize myself. But I'm not above trying.

Pick up the phone and talk like I'm crazy
Oh, there's something inside that stirs when I see you
I'll watch as every thread undoes itself
And when you come around
I'll nurse you back to pieces
...
Looking back tonight
I said, I said, I said...
I'll find your missing pieces
I'll love you back to pieces

Cathedrals, *Unbound*

Am I the Antagonist?

In the Reddit forum r/AmITheAsshole, readers submit confessions for public verdict. The post always unfolds in the same format: a situation, told sympathetically from the author's point of view, ending with the signature question. Often the author's tone contains a blend of righteous indignation and incredulity where the ending question—*Am I the asshole?*—can seem an afterthought, rhetorical because in their head, they've already made up their mind.

Readers then vote: YTA (yes); NTA (no); ESH (everyone sucks here); NAH (no assholes here). As one might expect from a massively online court where the jurors up-and-downvote, nuance rarely shines through. For most readers, the forum is the equivalent of the newspaper funnies of yore. Few posts ask for careful consideration because that's not what the OP (original poster) is there for. Some judicial readers reply INFO (need more information). Some question the story's rendering from an unreliable narrator. The system assumes villainy is judgeable and assignable, a label you either are or are not.

I spent three years certain I knew the villain in my story: he was the one who left.

Al-Anon is a Twelve Step program for the family and friends of alcoholics who are all affected by someone else's drinking. I came to the rooms in the aftermath of a romantic relationship to understand what happened to me—and then to assign blame and receive validation. Sound familiar? The program had other plans. Al-Anon is not about the alcoholic, despite its name. It's about everyone else, mainly me: my thinking, my patterns, and the ways I organized my life around managing someone else's dry drinking without even realizing that's what I was doing.

I developed a compulsive urge to solve Conor's problems, even without his asking, paving a path to what's called *learned helplessness*. From my perspective, I was a loving partner doing what loving partners do: loving him. From another perspective, I was managing him. The difference, once I saw the coin's other side, is hard to unsee. The simple diagnostic I use now came from a friend. I repeat two questions: Did anyone ask me? Am I the only one who can? The answer, embarrassingly enough, is often no, and no.

Step Four in the program involves taking a searching and fearless moral inventory. Step Five entails admitting the exact nature of my wrongs: to myself, to my Higher Power, to another human. Mine surfaced during a rite I participated in on retreat with this as the verdict: I couldn't say loving Conor was wrong. The problem was *how* I loved him—as a project, a proof to myself, a person to lavish upon what I couldn't yet give myself. I mistook his need for my rescue, earning for deserving. The grief that followed wasn't just for him. It was for every version of me who had learned to make the same mistakes before, over and over.

Step Eight tasks making a list of everyone I've harmed, with myself at the top. Step Nine asks me to make amends to them. The literature is clear on one aspect above all: do not expect amends from another. My stepwork is my own regardless of whether I receive one. I know this. I'm also still waiting—for an email, a phone call, a version of this story where he circles back. What my stepwork has turned up instead: a version of me who keeps reaching back, who reads every unanswered silence as an invitation to try harder, who believes this time will work—who gives himself secondhand cringe.

In the subreddit, the most argued-over submissions are those where the author is clearly the asshole but refuses to see it. Comments follow with readers explaining, gently, then not so gently, what the author has missed about their own story. Then, textbook denial. The entire thread unfolds as an anonymous tragedy. Public verdict rarely leads to self-insight. It arrives, if it ever does, through the slow work of looking hard and clear. AITA provides a crowdsourced service pointing where to look, but most often, the breadcrumbs lead back to the mirror and self we knew to be waiting there all along.

I'm on my fifth attempt at going through with Al-Anon. I know because my stack of newcomer welcome pamphlets over the years tallies the count. Each time, I came in thinking I knew what I was there for. Each time, the program waited patiently for me to discover I was wrong. The villain in my story is not the one who left, or at least, not the only one. It's also the one who loved selfishly and called it devotion; who helped without invitation and called it care; who built a future around someone else's healing and was surprised when it didn't hold.

I followed myself to the verdict in the mirror and have no desire to appeal. I'm not sure if that makes me hopeful or delusional. Probably both with the same coin again, another wish in the well.

And it's the same thing
You're repeating yourself and it's the same girl
Who's giving you hell
And it's the same face
Your heart keeps breaking in the same place

The Japanese House, *Something Has to Change*

prosopagnosia

Everyone looks familiar to me. We probably don't know each other, but I'll feel like we do. I may even tell you the story of your life, except it's not yours. Cut me off and tell me you're not who I think you are. I've heard it before. I've been wrong before, too—many times. It won't hurt my feelings, but it will help fine-tune how I recognize people without their faces.

Most explanations of prosopagnosia, more commonly known as faceblindness, include a visual showing heads with smooth, blank skin where facial features should be, or a distorted swirl in place of a face. That's not how it works for me. I can see the physical features that constitute a face. I could describe them well enough for a sketch artist to render an accurate portrait. I just can't connect them to the person or identity I know; it's recognition without identification. The face arrives—yet the name, the context, the relationship stay just out of reach, like a word that never resolves at the tip of the tongue.

When I was a kid, I had a magnet sheet with illustrated faces showing various faces and labels underneath: happy, sad, angry, confused, etc. A separate, movable frame read, *today I'm feeling*. The idea was to slot the frame over the face and emotion of the day and declare it, as an engaging emotional intelligence teaching tool. I treated it like a *Guess Who?* matching game, and that's how I learned. The faces, thankfully all of the same character, were legible; the feeling associated with the corresponding face was the part that didn't quite land.

I eventually learned to read faces through this kind of pattern matching. Years later, in college, a therapist handed me a printed version of the same chart. They had added more faces, more gradations of feelings as we had nuanced words for them. I told her I understood the system; I just wasn't sure it was describing anything I could reliably find inside myself.

Years later still, I learned to mimic, or rather contort, my face in the correct configuration to express the corresponding emotion I was feeling. I found my words were not as convincing to people, for whatever reason. I could not simply state my feelings for others to accept or believe. Many times, people would not react how I thought appropriate until I started crying from frustration and distress. Then it was suddenly a 5-alarm emergency. But why?

I would rather not reach the point of tears in the first place. Why couldn't they believe my words at face value?

Have you seen a 6'3 grown man cry? It's ugly and uncomfortable, and everyone wants to avoid it at all costs.

After electroconvulsive therapy, I developed a mild form of prosopagnosia. I used to have a sharp visual memory—useful for art history, making art, locking in a face across a crowded room and making strangers feel known. The faces from before the procedure remain relatively intact with the occasional blending or blurring as with anyone. Everyone since the procedure: familiar, more blurred, not readily placeable. I can't prove causation, but I'm thirty-five and have no other known brain trauma. I'm sure the risk was declared in the fine print on the forms I signed in the hospital. The timeline alone is enough for me. I didn't notice anything was wrong *enough* until I ended up in a stranger's home thinking I knew him.

Spoiler: I'm still alive.

I had met him, or so I thought, at a coffee shop in downtown Oakland. A week or so later, I received a Partiful invite for a breakfast potluck from a Nathan I didn't recognize. But the small circular avatar on the platform looked like the coffee shop manager. I assumed he countered and one-up invited me. I had invited him to my book launch for *Not in the Mood* at the Roxie, paired with a screening of Wong Kar-Wai's *In the Mood for Love* (2000). I was advertising exclusively via flyers because I still believe in print. My flyers had a QR code to the Partiful, and here was my invite to his. It was a logical conclusion.

I arrived at his home with Flamin' Hot Cheeto dust prepared to win the best oatmeal topping contest. My longtime answer to a Hinge dating app prompt, *Dating me is like...*, was lifted from a pineapple salsa at one of my favorite taco spots in the Los Feliz neighborhood of LA: *a French kiss but spicy*. Excellent skill, cutting and collaging across media, but I couldn't tell you what any of the men I dated looked like afterward.

The front door was unlocked. I made my way up to the top floor of a classic San Francisco Victorian, a hexagonal living room, bay window views out to the rest of the city. I introduced myself, made small talk. Another guest asked how I knew the hosts, Nathan and his roommates. I said I met Nathan at a coffee shop. *A real-life meet-cute*, I kept to myself. As the group conversation progressed, I gathered context clues that Nathan went to Brown with a few of the other guests. I thought it odd that he worked at a coffee shop, but quickly chastised myself—wasn't I myself trying to do what I wanted, not what was expected of me? I just as quickly pivoted to cheering him on.

When he and I found ourselves sitting next to each other, I asked how the coffee shop was going. He looked at me questioningly. *What coffee shop?* I specified: *in Oakland*. He still looked confused. My mind scrambled as I tried tracing back to what could have happened. I simultaneously started evaluating egress options. He doesn't work at a coffee shop in Oakland. Never has.

In day-to-day life I've developed workarounds to help me navigate life with people and faces. Unlike Miranda Priestly in *The Devil Wears Prada*, I don't have two assistants who whisper guests' identities in my ear at galas as they approach. Instead, I triangulate with hairstyle and height, voice and clothing as backup. Bridget, who volunteers with the liturgy at church, wears a white habit, bright dyed red hair, and a thick German accent. At coffee hour, without the habit, I still hesitate. Five seconds is all it takes, but it's enough to feel wrong. Now when I see someone vaguely familiar, which is often, I've started asking: do I look familiar? It sounds like a line because it is—but it also outsources recognition to someone whose brain can finish the job.

The night of my friend Jisun's book launch and after-party, I made three staggering mistakes in quick succession.

The first: Jisun works at my former employer, and I mistook a woman for my old coworker Brenda; we all present East Asian. When I registered the error and apologized, she laughed. She and Brenda both worked in the same building, she told me. It happened all the time. I felt shades of relief: both less face blind and less racist.

The second: a man across the room whose face I kept returning to. He looked like someone I'd dated—Josh, who had briefly moved to Sacramento, but still came to see me, whose grandmother lived near me at the time in the Marina. I asked if I looked familiar to him. He didn't know who I was or what I was talking about. I offered the details about Josh anyway, as evidence I wasn't making it up as an excuse to talk to him—which is exactly what someone making it up as an excuse would say. He and his girlfriend didn't continue to the after-party, but I needed redemption. I showed Josh's photo to another in the group to confirm the resemblance. He saw it. I wasn't making it up. He asked another mutual friend: *does this look like anyone we know who came to the book launch?* The mutual friend saw it, too, and answered, Daniel. I felt vindicated and also like a person who shows photos of strangers to other strangers at parties, which is exactly what I did. Stalker and serial killer behavior.

The third strike I already made once before. I met an Architecture and Design curator at a gallery across the street from the museum. Yosef looks exactly like a man I dated in Amsterdam. I looked him up on LinkedIn to confirm he hadn't fabricated an entire alternate identity with witness protection. Over a decade ago, he was at CCA. Tobias was in Amsterdam. They couldn't be the same person if both were true.

I've started to wonder if I have a type, or if my type is simply my brain misidentifying someone I previously loved, trying to bring them back.

Which brings me to the calling card.

In 2019, before any of this—before the break up, the aftermath, the treatments—I walked into a wine bar in Russian Hill and found a bartender I couldn't stop looking at. This was a problem, since I don't drink, and he was the only bartender, and the tiny space could only fit four seats. I couldn't act on the attraction directly; he was working a service role, the signals were ambiguous, and the context was wrong. Simply by being 6'3 with broad shoulders and walking in, I've cornered him without meaning to. I did what felt like the only classy move remaining: I slipped a calling card into his jacket pocket hanging nearby, and left without saying anything beyond polite inquiries into their nonalcoholic options. I told myself it was sophisticated, matchmaking but for myself. Taking matters into my own hands, *carpe diem*, YOLO, etc.

I never heard from him, and I moved on like I was in my twenties in a major city that introduces new people every day. I'm not keeping track since it doesn't matter until it does: I find the one. I found Conor a year later. We were together for three years through the pandemic and then some. I proposed; he counterproposed—with parting ways. He left to walk through a valley of his own, which is one way of saying he needed to leave, and I needed to let him. I've been in the aftermath ever since.

After Jisun's book launch, the after-party moved to Evil Eye in the Mission. I had met Dorian with Jisun at the Roxie's housewarming party to celebrate purchasing our building. We were mid-conversation, the kind of easy back-and-forth that made me think the night could go somewhere, when I asked where he was working that he couldn't come out the next Friday night. He named the wine bar that sounded eerily familiar. I kept my face neutral as I asked clarifying questions, all the while trying to sound casual: what neighborhood, the timeline, the interior. The details accumulated until I was certain. Then I asked, gingerly, whether he ever came across a calling card in his jacket pocket. He said he remembered it, might even still have it.

I stood there with a drink in my hand feeling paranoia and fear—not the potentially enjoyable, adrenaline kind, but one that opens doors to questions I'm not sure I want answered. Was this really the same man? At the Roxie party, I had asked if I looked familiar because he sure did. He listed off his usual haunts about town, and the only plausible match was his living in the Mission while I lived nearby in Mission Dolores. And here Dorian was again: familiar, unplaceable—until he wasn't. It didn't help that he also looked so much like Conor.

The prosopagnosia runs in every direction here, two trick mirrors placed across from each other, creating a distorted infinity. My brain couldn't retrieve his identity from his face, but another cognitive process had run the match without the neurons connecting to tell me. Whether that part of my brain recognized him, or the shape of what I'd wanted then and wanted again in Conor, I can't tell. Dorian is slightly lankier. The pull of the attraction is the same. Recognition without identification: the face arrives, but not the person behind it.

I still don't know who was who.

I put my head on my shoulders
Try to be someone, yeah
I tilt my person three degrees
To try to get along, yeah
It's so uncomfortable trying
To fit into this skin, yeah

Allie X, *Little Things*

in search of displaced time, a moonlit aftersun

I. The right book to the right reader at the right time

In one of my many brief forays in graduate studies, I learned about this library science principle coined by Francis K.W. Drury from his 1930 book, *Book Selection*. For me, the concept extends to all art and even to people with chance encounters: *the right teacher to the right seeker at the right time.*

I was fourteen when *Brokeback Mountain* (2005) came out and incredulous that Jake Gyllenhaal and Heath Ledger starred as gay cowboy lovers, supported by Michelle Williams and Anne Hathaway as their wives. Oscar award season rolled around, and it swept—winning Best Director, Adapted Screenplay, and Original Score, but not Best Picture. I had the audacity to immediately resent *Crash* for winning. *Crash*‽ The tragedy reminds me of James Baldwin writing *Giovanni's Room* with only white protagonists because the American public could only hold one form of oppression in its consciousness at a time. Eight years later, I finally watched *Brokeback Mountain* at my college friend's cottage on Lake Skaneateles after we had graduated. It crushed me, but I'm not sure I could've handled it at any point earlier. Similarly, I couldn't watch *Moonlight* (2016) until seven years after its release and discourse, nor *Aftersun* (2022).

This time delay isn't uniform, though. I watched *All of Us Strangers* (2023) immediately, twice, back to back at the Roxie, where I even snagged the movie poster as a minor board perk. I splurged on its framing, but now it's so heavy, I leave it leaning from the floor in my hallway because I don't trust mounting. The film adapts a Japanese ghost story featuring Andrew Scott and Paul Mescal as queer alienated neighbors in the same empty apartment building. Similar to the realization I wanted to date Scott, not just any priest, after *Fleabag* Season 2, my back to back Mescal nostalgia tour led me to realize I love all his characters, or maybe just him, see also *History of Sound* (2025) opposite Josh O'Connor.

II. How often in one lifetime can you recover from disappointment?

In *Starting from Scratch*, Andrea Marcolongo analyzes Virgil's *Aeneid* through the themes of new beginnings after upheaval. Aeneas's odyssey starts from the fall of his hometown Troy to what some claim as the founding of Rome, despite the four-century gap. I love the *Aeneid*'s themes of resiliency in the face of constant hardship and the enduring provisions of *pietas*, a sense of piety and duty. Marcolongo considers the epic poem essential reading for anyone who would rather not lay siege to a foreign city for ten years in the name of a woman and spend another ten years wandering home by sea. Fair—though I still went on my own odyssey, traveling far and wide in my twenties to see more of the world, and also in search of a culture and society that might better fit someone who values relationships in community over material ambition or career success. Unfortunately for me, the challenge of modernity has spread equally far and wide. More recently I've started to wonder—maybe I need to search across time.

Last year, I went to an author talk organized by Two Lines Press for Elena Garro's *The Week of Colors*, a collection of her short stories translated by Megan McDowell, and Jazmina Barrera's *The Queen of Swords*, an investigation into Garro's enigmatic life. I was intrigued by McDowell and Barrera's comments on how Garro experienced time: nonlinearly. I wanted to better understand what they meant and if they had any firsthand accounts from her journals, which Barrera combed through in the Garro archives at Princeton. They said the best examples come from her fiction, specifically the first story, which was the only one I quickly skimmed beforehand in my advanced copy I received from fanboying. I must have low skimming comprehension since their account varied widely from my own understanding, especially from missing the time jumps across centuries.

In this vein, I thought I might jump a century or so myself to Marcel Proust (1871–1922). While I've only read a bit of *Swann's Way*, I've read analyses on what he does in the series, and I don't care for it; or rather, for me, *the juice ain't worth the squeeze*. This was a heavy point of contention in my last relationship, to the point of breaking up initially due to differences in interpreting art, but I stand by my take. I'm glad he eventually came around to my points of view to celebrate diversity in art reception, to access different doors leading to the same room, and to cringe from *Paterson* (2016); he never conceded the last. I shelve Proust with *Infinite Jest*, *Solenoid*, and Knausgård's *My Struggle* in a section titled dickmanifestos-by-men-who-need-help. Then one day on my daily trip to the library, I came across a slim collection of Proust's nine rediscovered short stories, published in English as *The Mysterious Correspondent*. I have a weakness for epistles, especially in fiction. I love the heightened, time-delayed, drama!

One of my favorite stories in the collection, *Gift of the Fairies*, describes a common tale that resonates:

You will suffer, though, since to their gifts I must, alas!, join my own. I am the fairy of misunderstood sensitivities. Everyone will harm you, the ones you won't love, the ones you will love even more. ...your body will not resist the repercussions of the impulses and matters of your heart. You will often be feverish. You will not sleep, you will be constantly shivering.

While my mood disorder manifests the overload of feelings primarily in my head, the visceral responses in the body remind me of the prophets — jumping across a couple millennia — as Abraham Heschel describes them: *The prophet is a man who feels fiercely. God has thrust a burden upon his soul...* But perhaps Jeremiah says it best himself, *...there is in my heart as it were a burning fire shut up in my bones, and I am weary with holding it in, and I cannot.* I love the closing clause, *and I cannot*. I also appreciate how Heschel emphasizes the prophet is still a man, human with his own personality, fallibility, moods:

The prophet is a person, not a microphone. He is endowed with a mission...but also with temperament, concern, character, and individuality. As there was no resisting the impact of divine inspiration, so at times there was no resisting the vortex of his own temperament.

I can barely handle my own moods, let alone divine pathos, so I additionally admire the prophet's ability to delineate God's righteousness from his own.

This dissatisfaction with the status quo and normativity of the masses carries through the centuries, if not on moral religious grounds, then at least still through academic discourse. Danish theologian and existential philosopher Søren Kierkegaard (1813–1855) wrote in ways I would describe simply as sassy—a young man's slow-dawning laughter at everything his world said he should strive for: a judgeship, a well-off wife, God reduced to communion once a year. A similar sentiment pops up half a century later, across the world, in Japanese novelist Natsume Sōseki's (1867–1916) *And Then*, where the protagonist Daisuke comments with profound detachment:

Look at society: everyone is running around frantically, competing and exhausting themselves for the sake of survival, and they call this 'civilization.' In reality, they've just become slaves to their livelihoods.

Replace survival with status, and the line still holds for most of my milieu.

I feel a fellowship with these likeminded writers, but I find them few and far between. I'd like to find more in the here and now. I finished Patrick Anderson's *The Lamentations* on queer suicides, where he blends personal stories and public histories, of those who searched for the universal desire to love and be loved, yet were rebuffed, scorned, and detested by those around them. I still believe suicide is a symptom of societal failure. As Heschel says, *Above all, the prophets remind us of the moral state of a people: Few are guilty, but all are responsible.* Brain chemistry deviates naturally, but any society with suicide has a severe, collective problem.

Heike Bauer in *The Hirschfeld Archives* unpacks what remains of the case studies and archival records compiled by Magnus Hirschfeld, a pioneering German sexologist. Hirschfeld centered the understanding of queer, transgender, and gender-nonconforming individuals' lived experiences in the early 1900s, in a field that would have otherwise rejected these lives as deviance. He founded the Institute for Sexual Science in Berlin in 1919, but shortly after, the Nazi-led German Student Union ransacked it in 1933 and publicly burned its massive archives on the Opernplatz. Bauer describes what survived as a record of suffering that left little trace yet still reverberates, still haunts.

I feel this haunting. But not solely through queerness. As many friends know, I have no problem calling out offenses, grievances, or injustice. I'm less gifted in the follow-through for persuasion and effecting lasting change. That said, I don't see myself lacking in prophetic vision or imagination. Every now and then, though, the darkness grows darker, *and I cannot*. A close friend distilled the anguish I was feeling into this insight:

Thank you for trusting me with this. Underneath all of it, what I hear is how badly you want to be chosen the way you choose people. To be the one someone plans for and thinks of without having to be asked. Wanting that is fair. It's most of what any of us are really after, and you give it so generously, so of course its absence lands as hard as it does.

I don't want solely to be chosen by a romantic partner, though I understand most people do and stop there. It certainly helps; but I'm frustrated with the staggering drops with which people treat their friends in comparison. I prioritize my limited time and energy like everyone else, but my bands are much closer together. Another close friend pointed out that those of us blessed with mothers who loved us deeply and taught us how to love by example will have a much harder time finding a similar, reciprocal love in the outside world. I'm seeing more and more how love can take the form of a double edged sword.

In this darkness, I think of James Baldwin's essay *Nothing Personal*:

One discovers the light in darkness, that is what darkness is for... It is necessary, while in darkness, to know that there is a light somewhere, to know that in oneself, waiting to be found, there is a light.

This can be hard to remember in the shadows. Earlier this year, I found an essay my ex wrote and shared long ago. I wanted to share it back to him, drafted an email, and never sent it:

I'm sending this because I thought you might like to hear from yourself, because sometimes we give parts of ourselves to others to hold onto and share back to us when we need...Of course, I remember reading the essay, but different parts of it stood out to me this time. Perhaps you'd like to reflect on, and celebrate, how far you've come from then, and the many thens before.

III. Luce caelesti in paradisum ictus

In the words of Canadian indie band Wolf Parade, can anyone *give me your eyes / I need sunshine*? How does this situation change, how do I bring the future I want into the present? I had lunch with a friend's twenty-four year old son who seemed precociously mature in accepting his nature, even as tiring and difficult as he found it in relation to the world around him. I felt a resonance, but a decade ahead of him, and I'm weary. In *Aftersun*, Mescal's character Calum shares, *I can't see myself at forty, to be honest. Surprised I made it to thirty*, as he turns thirty-one, and as the film implies, takes his life shortly after. I remember feeling similarly in my twenties, pleasantly surprised I made it to thirty, though seemingly losing steam at thirty-five—especially seeing my friend's spritely eighty-three year old aunt. *I can't see myself at forty, to be honest.*

Last year, a new close friend invited me to a New Year's event creating bingo cards as vision boards. Shortly after the midpoint of the year, I only have three squares left, but I think they are the hardest: *gelâzenheit*, let it unfold; make magic; and see without eyes. I want to see, I want to believe, and I want to be seized, like the father seized by hope, by life, by the power of God, as he begs Jesus to heal his son, in Fleming Rutledge's account in *Help My Unbelief*. As she says, *The instant is electric.* Like Ted Chiang's characters in *Hell Is the Absence of God* who are struck by Heaven's light and blinded by a devotion that vanquishes doubt. Grant me vision to see what eyes cannot. *Seize my unbelief.*

IV. Dilexi te

Stop all the clocks—I'm displaced in the wrong time. But every now and then, I'm given a visual to crystallize what I'm feeling and tide me over. This one stems in part from a collage I made of the Louvre and *Mona Lisa*, specifically framed by the rough tears of the paper's edges. Another aspect comes from a tattoo a pastor wanted: a leap of faith represented by a human figure swan diving from the index finger of Adam to God from Michelangelo's *The Creation of Adam* (1510) fresco in the Sistine Chapel. My vision has a cropped closeup of an arm that reaches from above and a hand that grasps the forearm from below, vice versa, locked in embrace. Recall *The*

Matrix: Morpheus breaks free from his handcuffs on an interrogation floor in the federal building, runs across to escape, gets shot near the edge, stumbles yet still trapeze-leaps for Neo, and hangs by a single limb off Neo's arm in a flying helicopter—*a leap of faith*. My own leap calls through a tear in space, a wrinkle in time.

Anderson ends his requiem with an overview of Andrew Holleran's novel *Dancer from the Dance* (1978):

...the story of Malone, a beautiful young gay man who entrances the countless other gay men who populate the queer spaces of New York nightlife of the era: the bars, clubs, bathhouses, parks, and back alleys in which queer life was lived... he is ultimately driven by his desire to find a man with whom he can nurture a deep and abiding love. This he does not find; "We're completely free," he comments to a friend in a park while cruising one night, "and that's the horror."

We're not at all completely free, not all of us anyway, but that's another essay. Anderson specifically cites the closing letter:

The final letter—which, unlike all of the others, is signed not with a campy pseudonym but with its author's actual name, Paul—muses on the queer scene of the early and middle 1970s, the subterranean parties and sweaty club nights and other ecstasies that had felt so much like freedom... "Love, in the best of circumstances, is hard to find," Paul writes, before urging his friend to "mourn no longer for Malone...Go out dancing tonight, my dear, and go home with someone, and if the love doesn't last beyond the morning, then know I love you."

I find it fascinating that Anderson titled his book *Lamentations*, a book in the Old Testament mourning the fall of Jerusalem, and subtitled it a requiem, a specific Mass in the Catholic Church for the recently deceased, yet did not comment on what calls out clearly to me as a mirroring of the Apostle Paul's epistles and separately Revelation 3:9. This verse grounds Pope Leo's *Dilexi Te* (2025), the title of which is Latin for *I have loved you*. In it, Christ proclaims to a small, marginalized Christian community treated with contempt by those surrounding them: regardless of how the world treats you, know that I have loved you. These are words I still need to hear in San Francisco in 2026.

In the seemingly small faction, where subterranean parties and sweaty club nights and other ecstasies do not feel like freedom, I instead feel alien. I'm bombarded by advertising, media, social media for what I should want, yet I find myself returning to these lines from *The Devil Wears Prada*: *But what if this isn't what I want? I mean, what if I don't want to live the way you live?*

Pray for me.

We're only young and naive still
We require certain skills
The mood it changes like the wind
Hard to control when it begins
The bittersweet between my teeth
Trying to find the in-betweens

The Naked and Famous, *Young Blood*

Paying to Exist

Darkness isn't empty—it has depth. Similarly, a hole is not a void; it has boundaries. The difference between one kind of life and another can be barely noticeable to the outside eye but the membrane between them, thin and porous enough to feel the draft. In 2008, I was seventeen, and the global financial markets were collapsing in ways that would reshape an economy I'd spend years trying to enter, then survive, then leave, stage right.

After bouts of depressions, barely finishing high school and college as a result, the first time I experienced euphoria was visiting San Francisco during the last days of summer before graduate school. My body was electric: jittery, wide awake without sleep, ready to walk laps up and down the city. I didn't know what was happening but I liked it. I talked nonstop at a stranger on a plane for four hours. Back home I still couldn't sleep. I filled sketchbooks, texted uncontrollably, saw visions: interpretations of Genesis, paranoia around an alum I met for coffee believing he was Satan incarnate. I cognitively knew none of this was real in terms of facts. It was also the most vivid reality I had ever felt as true.

One psychiatrist wanted to medicate me immediately. Another congratulated me on a hyperthymic temperament. I liked his verdict better and left his office in validated spirits. I moved to Paris instead of attending graduate school, absconding with my scholarship. I rented a former maid's quarters on the top floor of a Haussmann building in the 7th, fell asleep in classic cinemas, wrote bad poetry. After four months in some side of paradise, a mugging outside a literary wine bar dispelled the magic. Depression came for me like winter's barren reaper.

My parents welcomed me back like the Prodigal Son. What I hadn't yet understood was that the arc I'd just traced—elevation, expansion, collapse—would become the defining rhythm of my next decade.

I joined Google the following year. Again, I had boundless productivity, sleepless nights, and a foul irritability. The hypomanic episode was untenable and, after four months again, ended in a dramatic crash. Euphoria always has a price.

Over the years that followed, I encountered the new forms my mind could take: hypomania without euphoria, only irritability; stretches of hypomania lasting a full year; depression so severe it required electroconvulsive therapy. My providers now think the psychotic symptoms warrant a Bipolar I diagnosis. The disorder overlaps with schizophrenia and epilepsy in sharing a common underlying pathway. The brain remains a vast, murky mystery, and medicine has come a long way from lobotomy, though not far enough.

Throughout my employment, I took multiple disability leaves, sometimes one every year or two. They cost me promotions, raises, credibility that only accumulates through consistent presence. The American workplace doesn't have an arrangement for a body and mind that periodically needs to stop. It welcomes overdrive, but not interruption. What it has instead is an accommodation process: a formal structure designed to protect the company more than the employee. The demands don't disappear; they sublimate into paperwork for consistency, reliability, and affordability.

Eventually, I wasn't. I was let go after a decade.

Over a century ago, Max Weber identified what he called the Protestant work ethic: not merely people working hard, but work assuming a specifically moral character. To waste time was not just inefficiency or luxury, but a moral failing. I've thought about this often while lying in a dark room during a depressive episode, failing. The ambient shame, the sense that I was not just unwell but also somehow worthless, took years to recognize as a cultural judgment rather than personal. Work had become, as Weber observed, a form of worship, and what I was doing was heretical. When the layoff came, the insurance went with it.

Reconstructing a care team through Medi-Cal including a psychiatrist, therapist, and primary care physician meant navigating referral chains, prior authorization requests, intake interview after intake interview, and providers listed as in network but haven't accepted new patients in years. The additional labor becomes a second job: calling, waiting, repeating my history, proving need in formats legible to bureaucracies. A pharmacy delayed a mood stabilizer for eleven days. I have the time, cognitive capacity, and family safety net that keeps me housed while I wait. I know what it looks like when someone doesn't.

I've walked the sidewalks of San Francisco for over a decade and become viscerally aware of how only a thin membrane separates me from my unhoused neighbors. On any given block in the Mission, SoMa, or the Tenderloin, I see people whose conditions may not be so different from mine, but whose insurance, family resources, race, or even simply the timing of their first episode, were different enough to matter completely.

The membrane is permeable. I've felt the draft come through.

The threshold is purely procedural. A missed appointment. A form not processed in time. A prescription delayed eleven days. An episode that arrives before the healthcare system catches up. A gap in coverage becomes a gap in care becomes a gap in functioning becomes a gap in employment becomes a gap in housing. None of this is unusual nor accidental. The membrane is maintained through strict thresholds: eligibility requirements, documentation standards, timelines assuming capability and continuity. To remain on the right side requires at minimum, the appearance of stability, sustained over time.

So far, I've managed to remain legible enough to the system. I know how contingent my precarious position is: determined by a series of decisions made by other people, often far away, about what counts as need and stability. A form filled out correctly, signed or unsigned. A diagnosis coded this way instead of that.

As one guide for providers states, *bipolar disorder carries the most structurally complex code family in behavioral health*: *ICD-10-CM* [diagnostic coding system for insurance] *crosses current episode type × severity × psychotic features × remission status.*

31.0	Bipolar disorder, current episode hypomanic
31.10	Bipolar disorder, current episode manic without psychotic features, unspecified
31.11-3	Bipolar disorder, current episode manic without psychotic features, mild / moderate / severe without psychotic features
31.2	Bipolar disorder, current episode manic severe with psychotic features
31.30	Bipolar disorder, current episode depressed, mild or moderate severity, unspecified
31.31-3	Bipolar disorder, current episode depressed, mild / moderate / severe without psychotic features

31.4 Bipolar disorder, current episode depressed, severe, without psychotic features
31.5 Bipolar disorder, current episode depressed, severe, with psychotic features
31.60 Bipolar disorder, current episode mixed, unspecified
31.61-3 Bipolar disorder, current episode mixed, mild / moderate / severe without psychotic features
31.64 Bipolar disorder, current episode mixed, severe, with psychotic features
31.70 Currently in remission, most recent episode unspecified
31.71 In partial remission, most recent episode hypomanic
31.72 In full remission, most recent episode hypomanic
31.73 In partial remission, most recent episode manic
31.74 In full remission, most recent episode manic
31.75 In partial remission, most recent episode depressed
31.76 In full remission, most recent episode depressed
31.77 In partial remission, most recent episode mixed
31.78 In full remission, most recent episode mixed

A provider willing to take on a patient whose history suggests more work than they want.

Legibility to bureaucracy is its own kind of labor and performance. It requires presenting a version of myself that can be easily processed, like a Scantron: coherent, compliant, improving. It means knowing which parts of my experience translate into bureaucratic-speak beneficially and which do not. Too much volatility reads as risk, too much stability disqualifies care. I've learned over time how to calibrate: how to read as unwell enough to qualify, but well enough to manage the process. All this navigation and calibration is rarely acknowledged as labor. At best, nonprofits call it self-advocacy. No record of it exists in medical records except by proxy, but it means the difference between remaining inside the membrane and falling through it.

Housing is most Americans' largest recurring expense. During the pandemic, the City and County of San Francisco allocated $61,000 per year per tent in encampments. Its annual budget exceeds $13 billion, and the State of California recently posted a $100 billion surplus. The gap between what these numbers claim and what the sidewalks show is offensive and by design. The structural preferences, decisions made over and over by those in power, perpetuate the divide between whose existence is a problem to be managed and contained—and whose life is worth enriching and sustaining.

I've been paying rent in one of the world's most expensive cities for over a decade. I remember finding the concept of rent so strange when I first encountered it as a teenager. I understood purchasing, a one time transaction to pay for what you want. Paying perpetually, with no equity and no end, for the right to occupy a space someone else owns—that was a different logic and a hard pill to swallow. I refused and looked for the cheapest rent-to-quality ratio I could find. My first room in San Francisco was $1,100—a lofted space above the living room, no enclosing walls and no door. My second was $1,300, shared with the senior landlady and her partner whom I jokingly called my grandparents. In 2018, I splurged on a Marina studio at $2,250, where I was effectively head of DEI for the neighborhood. A couple of pandemic apartments later, I paid $1,300 again for a room in an apartment that's rent controlled and "mine" only in the sense that it's leased, month to month, at someone else's pleasure.

The housing market is a set of choices by legislators, investors, landlords, and zoning boards that benefit themselves and the landowning class. Nothing about any market is natural in the sense of naturally occuring; it's constructed. The language of affordability performs useful ideological work here since it attributes rising rents to impersonal forces, say an *invisible hand*, rather than to decisions made by specific people in specific rooms for their own benefit. For example: restrict supply, watch bidding wars, reap more and more profit.

Consumer goods like bananas spoil or become obsolete; a landlord holding an empty apartment in a rising market is making money in absolute terms, even without a tenant. There will always be demand for shelter—that's its greatest leverage.

I'm not a homeowner and do not intend to become one. In certain American registers, this decision is further heresy against the Dream. A mortgage is not compatible with the life I want to live—one that can stop when it has to, that can rest, that cannot be foreclosed from a depressive episode. Homeowners with large mortgages are not as free to take disability leaves, or choose lower-paying work, or refuse a dangerous environment because they need the insurance. I've chosen, deliberately, another form of entrapment that at least leaves me most mobile.

I've come to understand housing more as a test of capability, administered continuously, with little margin for interruption. There is no pause, rest, or reset, yet the most effective way to keep people housed is to provide assistance to keep them in their current housing. What appears from the outside as individual failure is often the known outcome of a system that does not accommodate variance.

After my relationship with Conor, I returned to Al-Anon again. I used to think progress required constant motion through the steps. Now I know rest is also progress—better, even, than spinning my wheels going nowhere. I've taken disability leaves, lost friends, and recently, my job. But I've gained, at considerable cost, a new kind of freedom.

Viktor Frankl, reflecting on surviving the Holocaust, said, *Instead of possibilities, I have realities—work done, love loved*. I spent years trying to build a life out of possibility alone, out of what could be, what might return. I want the other side now, the solidity of realities over what-ifs.

I've been walking these San Francisco sidewalks for over a decade and have felt the permeable membrane. I know which side I'm on, and I know it's not solely a matter of character. The systems that were meant to hold me—employment, insurance, housing, nonprofit infrastructure are working as designed, for someone. Not always for me. Almost never for the people I see on the other side.

What I have left, after the job and the relationship and several losses in my neurochemistry, is a care team I fought to assemble against a bureaucracy that would have let me slip; a room of my own to rest in; a set of rituals including morning walks around the park, stops at the Harvey Milk branch library, Saturday evenings at the Roxie; that all constitute, in aggregate, a life.

It's slower than what I once imagined my life would be. It's smaller, too, in certain ways. It doesn't resemble the trajectories I was conditioned to pursue or the ones I once believed I deserved. But it's durable; it holds.

The membrane is proof that care hasn't enveloped everyone yet. I'm on one side, still here, still watching. So is everyone on the other side—whether or not the system bothers to look.

Love, let's talk about love
Is it anything and everything you hoped for?
Or do the feeling haunt you? (Haunt)
I know the feeling haunt you (Haunt)

This may be the night that my dreams might let me know
All the stars approach you
All the stars approach you
All the stars approach you

This may be the night that my dreams might let me know
All the stars are closer
All the stars are closer
All the stars are closer

Kendrick Lamar & SZA, *All the Stars*

Mission Cassini

inner spirit, outer space

You, sent out beyond your recall,
go to the limits of your longing.
Embody me.

Flare up like a flame
and make big shadows I can move in.

Let everything happen to you: beauty and terror.
Just keep going. No feeling is final.

—Rilke, *Book of Hours I, 59*

NASA's Cassini space mission to Saturn launched from Cape Canaveral in October 1997. The combined weight of the Cassini orbiter and the European Space Agency's Huygens probe, along with the fuel needed for the vast distance, came out to two million pounds—much too heavy for a regular shuttle. The solution was Solid Rocket Motor Upgrades, the classic white boosters on the sides of rockets seen at launch. They provided the massive thrust needed to blast the load out of gravity's strongest pull and the atmosphere. On a televised launch, viewers can see these boosters burn out after about two minutes, detach, and fall back into the ocean.

The heavy-lift Titan IVB rocket then kicked in with its main stages to continue out of Earth's gravity. As each stage consumed its fuel, it fell off to reduce weight and disintegrated upon reentry. Stage 3, the Centaur upper stage, fired its engines to accelerate Cassini into the escape velocity needed to break from Earth's gravity entirely. Outside the gravity well, the Centaur detached into solar orbit as Cassini continued on its seven-year journey to Saturn, alone.

I first learned about light's dual existence as both wave and particle in my Modern Physics class at a public boarding school *Wired* called Hogwarts for Hackers. *How could light, let alone any matter, be both?* I wondered. Ingenious experimentation proved this reconciliation of seeming contradictions, which further explained the universe while keeping it intact. *Could I, too, be both?*

We learned that if the stars were infinite, their light would fill the night sky. Yet we see darkness. My preferred solution to Olbers' paradox: perhaps the stars' infinities just haven't reached us yet. I was that spacey student more comfortable with my head in cosmic clouds of stardust.

These lines of inquiry gave me the language to ponder the mysteries up above and deep within. A swirling spiral galaxy could represent my inner contradictions: queer and Christian, manic and depressive, not obviously white and not fully not-white. The unspooling nebula contains opposites I couldn't reconcile, yet refused to discard. I hold space in both hands, palms open, for whatever might come: a missing ingredient to tie it all together, like a unified theory of quantum gravity or time. Either could work.

Conor was my Centaur upper stage. He didn't do the initial heavy lifting of raising me into adulthood or forming my spirit, but he took me out of Earth's orbit. I had early stirrings I wasn't made for this world in its current iteration. When I was twenty-six, I circled back to my faith and found a church starting a LGBTQ+ reflection group led by two queer priests. After testing the waters, I prayed for a deeper faith and transformation. Three years later, I met Conor. He doesn't know it, but he took me out of this world. With a clearer view of the stars, the moon, and Earth below, I thought, *This is it, this must be the place*. But we didn't stay in orbit long. He launched me further than I wanted to go with the brute force needed to reach escape velocity. After the Trans Planetary Injection burn, he couldn't continue—intentional or not, he was spent. He detached into solar orbit, leaving me in a vacuum with no stars.

Conor wasn't the first to send me to my limits. A boy named Davis was the first person I fell in love with: February 2008 at boarding school. Off-campus, the global financial markets were roiling, but my world revolved around his eyes: emerald with a ring of orange fire. First love at seventeen was a rapture; pure, untested by reality, it stays with me still. Rebecca Solnit writes that all one's creation is done in that first decade and a half, when an internal landscape forms with the force of primordial volcanoes and plate tectonics. For me, it works just as well informed by my gaze upward: an internal cosmos forming with the force of exploding stars and gravity collapsing onto itself. Sometimes I feel I'm wandering the same spiral labyrinth formed in those developmental years, over and over, looking for those same iridescent eyes, the flashing ones that saw through my shadows.

Cassini's target was Saturn. Yet it launched toward the opposite direction, to Venus. The spacecraft needed more velocity than any technology on Earth could provide, so the mission looked to the planets. By flying into Venus's gravitational pull, Cassini accelerated, then swung by and hitched a ride on the planet's orbital momentum relative to the sun. Cassini's speed relative to Venus stayed the same before and after the flyby, but its speed relative to the sun increased since Venus is also orbiting the sun at the same time. The physics works. Cassini then looped around the sun for fourteen months while Venus did two smaller laps of its own. They met again at the same spot, and this time, the speed and angle let Cassini swing harder. After the second gravity assist, its orbit could reach all the way out to Jupiter. *Sometimes it feels like I'm going in circles, hoping to get somewhere, somehow.*

En route to Jupiter, Cassini swung back to Earth in August 1999—close to where it started, nearly two years earlier. Sometimes we go in the wrong direction just to come back to where we started and go even further in yet another direction. On repeat. Cassini used our own planet for a third gravity assist to reach Saturn. At least Cassini knew its target.

My first manic episode arrived the summer before graduate school with visions vivid enough to see two realities competing for dominance in my head at once. I've described this elsewhere in this book. What matters here is what I did with it afterward.

Many cultures once labeled *primitive* by the North Atlantic never demonized loving another person on the basis of sex. Further, what some cultures called mental illness, many honored as vision. I've learned to live with a disability. I've also learned to hold open the question of what it means that my mind can thin the boundaries keeping realities separate, allowing a translucency in between—visions can feel truer than waking life; *beauty and terror* arrive together, inseparable.

The medieval mystic Walter Hilton and later the anonymous author of *The Cloud of Unknowing*, described their approach to God as entering a cloud, irreducible unknowing, a place where ordinary knowing breaks down and another dimension begins. Modern physics offers an uncanny nanoscale parallel: the electron cloud, a probability distribution around the nucleus describing where the electron can most likely be found. One cannot know its exact position since the act of measuring changes the position. The cloud is the most accurate map representation of a particle that resists precise knowing. Perhaps my mind works similarly, and perhaps that's by design. The visions may not be knowledge, as we understand it. They were the cloud, a probability distribution of the sacred, transmitted from an unknown source, real like light as a wave before one measures, when it then decides to present as a particle.

Seven years after launch, three gravity assists from two different planets, through the asteroid belt, passed Jupiter—Cassini reached Saturn in July 2004. It arrived, not depleted, but with intention, enough fuel, and instruments intact to start the real mission: orbit Saturn for thirteen years, transmitting data no one had ever seen. Rings, 274 moons, a peculiar hexagonal jet stream at its north pole home to a six-sided geometric storm the size of three Earths, formed by uninterrupted wind and atmospheric pressure scientists still don't fully understand. Cassini transmitted without understanding; it just kept going.

I'm somewhere on that thirteen-year orbit. I don't know which loop I'm on, but I know I'm still transmitting. What I've encountered, rings I didn't expect, moons I couldn't name. Proof that I went this far and found it worth reporting.

After Conor detached, I drifted in a vacuum longer than I want to admit. When it came time to ritualize a commitment of forever together, he disclosed he needed to walk through a valley on his own. I could feel every part of me screaming *Don't leave me*. Nothing has been harder than letting him go.

What I hadn't understood was my confusing his gravity for my destination. He was a Centaur stage, a booster, not Saturn. The assist was real. The arrival was not. I developed a compulsive urge to solve his problems without his asking, mistaking rescue for care, jet propulsion for love. It's been years since my last contact with him. The Apostle Paul writes that devotion without distraction is its own, even more desirable offering. I'm not there yet. All around me, American culture glorifies coupling, and San Francisco prides itself on equality—for coupling—but neither honors, let alone understands, chosen solitude.

Go to the limits of your longing. I went, and I wanted to arrive at a destination where I could stay and rest, like a day spa for my spirit. Instead, I was pushed past the limits to where they became my thresholds: liminal limerence where I spent far too long sliding on an asymptote, getting closer, but never quite reaching.

Cassini's *Grand Finale* started in April 2017. Knowing the spacecraft's fuel was nearly exhausted, mission scientists made a deliberate choice: rather than let Cassini drift and potentially contaminate Saturn's moons, some of which may harbor conditions for life, they directed it into Saturn's atmosphere to *flare up like a flame*. Twenty-two times, Cassini threaded the gap between the planet and its innermost ring, a place no spacecraft had ever entered, transmitting data until the signal went dark on September 15, 2017. It blazed cosmic trails and kept transmitting until it immolated completely.

I think about that choosing often. The transmission until the last moment. The singular dedication to the mission. In Rilke's poem, the address sends someone out, urged to embody the sender, to let everything happen. I read the lines as what it means to be sent into this world with a body and mind that opens onto other planes and thins membranes; a heart that keeps loving past the point of reason. To *just keep going*. The promise of *no feeling is final.*

I'll never be an astronaut. That dream was foreclosed early: in the first episode of *The Magic School Bus*, Arnold takes off his helmet on Pluto, and his head flash-freezes into ice blocks. But I can always make-believe. The autumn I lived in Paris, my costume was a Daft Punk cosmonaut: a galaxy-infused glow-in-the-dark onesie and a vantablack motorcycle helmet. My fully grown adult, 6'3" self, feeling haughty and chic in the City of Lights. *Beauty*, gazing at the galaxies, and *terror*, suffocating in an unsecured airlock. Astronaut, or reluctant probe?

I don't want to go, but I know, in my own way, what it's like to be launched by forces greater than myself, assisted by bodies whose gravity I borrowed without fully understanding, traveling in the wrong direction more than once to eventually go further. Still transmitting. Still in orbit. Still searching for what I can't yet name, sending back my observations on rings, moons, dust.

[Transmission received: September 15, 2017. Location: 9.4° N, 53° W, Saturn.] The light is no mystery. The mystery is what keeps the light from passing through.

PS. Remember, *I have loved you*.

III. Coda

It's gone too far to ever go back
You know I wouldn't give you up but, baby, I don't want that
It hits you so hard to be so good
You know you keep so still and maybe it's a kind of flak

Maybe it's the reason that I'm back
Maybe it's alright
Maybe I've always been this kind
Baby, it's too hard, I'm too scarred for this to work again
But you know I still wake up with you every morning like I'm still dead

The Japanese House, *Still*

Pressure pushin' down on me
Pressin' down on you,
...
That's the terror of knowing what this world is about
...
And love dares you

David Bowie & Queen, *Under Pressure*

Discernment Under Pressure

Giving Beauty Its Shape

Discernment led me to this Literature & Spirituality seminar at the Jesuit School of Theology, and I want to continue exploring the topic as a lens through our readings this semester. After reading Pope Francis's letter *On the Role of Literature in Formation*, particularly his reference to Saint Paul VI's plea to artists and writers, I felt assured of both the class and my place in it. That assurance quickly faltered when we turned to our first novel, *The Book of Daniel*. What unsettled me was not simply my reaction to the text, but what it implied about my presence in the class at all. *I've been wrong before*, I muttered to myself, a phrase I'm well acquainted with.

That same weekend, after seriously considering dropping the class, I attended an Ignatian discernment retreat at St. Columba's in Inverness. During one session in the retreat house library, a sentence arrived in my mind phrased in a register I do not usually think to myself in: *I want you to write*. I hardly have a verbal inner dialogue. Most of the time my inner landscape is nebulous emotion and imagery. When I do think in words, they're singular in descriptors, like *hungry*. They're rarely strung together to form complete sentences, and they certainly don't start with *I want*. *Want* is a feeling word I keep strictly in the abstract, never naming, despite Rev. Erin, the retreat's organizer, insisting on the power of specificity in discernment and prayer. If I do talk to myself, it's in the simple imperative: *get up, come on, just do it*.

During a break in the same session, I came across Mary Oliver's *Upstream* jutting out from a shelf, almost calling to me. I was struck by how closely it resembled the cover of *The Wilderness That Bears Your Name*, from which I had read *How to Listen* as an opening prayer in class.

The main book that has shaped my thinking on discernment thus far is Henri Nouwen's *Discernment: Reading the Signs of Daily Life*, where he writes, "God speaks to us all the time and in many ways, but it requires spiritual discernment to hear God's voice, see what God sees, and read the signs in daily life." He names books, nature, people, and events among these channels. I felt lucky that *books* appeared on the list since *nature* has mostly met me with silence. Last April, I renamed my Substack from *Asking for a*

Friend to *ghost in the shelf*. At the time, I described the decision this way: "What I like about the name is when I ask God to speak to me, I have a few go-to channels to hear him. One of them is through books. I go to a bookstore or library and hope one catches my eye, or falls in front of me. ... I imagine a specific *Interstellar* (2014) scene, except instead of Matthew McConaughey and fifth-dimensional beings in a tesseract, it's a *ghost in the shelf*."

What happened at St. Columba's was a repetition of what I've already been experiencing. On the drive back to San Francisco, I decided to stay in the class. When I picked up *Upstream* at SFPL, I found passages that gave language to how I felt about creativity and writing. Again, I felt assured I was moving in the right direction. But assurance, I've learned, can be fleeting. The breadcrumbs were only visible because I was lost enough to need them, and the literature that followed kept teaching me this. Discernment stopped feeling like choosing between good options and began feeling like what remains when the field narrows. A narrower field might not make choice easier, but it does clarify the contours.

I began to recognize this paradox in James Baldwin's short story, *Sonny's Blues*. Sonny has no options in the conventional sense: he's constrained by incarceration, addiction, and midcentury Harlem as a young Black man. The story shows how expression takes shape through these constraints, without neat resolution. The image I envision is flowers pushing through cracks in concrete, similar to how a florist told me, when asked about her favorite flowers, she replied: *ditch flowers*. These were a subcategory of the more canonical wild flowers but thrive in the forsaken margins.

Sonny has one form available to him, music, and he inhabits it fully. Instead of choosing among possibilities, he's working within what remains. For most of the story, his brother, the story's narrator, tries to understand him through a framework that prioritizes stability and responsibility. What finally shifts his view is listening to Sonny play, not argument or persuasion.

I'm not asking you / to hold me together. / I'm asking you / to open so wide / there's room for all the ways / I come apart. —*How to Listen*.

In the final scene, understanding arrives through pure sound over explanation. The music renders Sonny's suffering legible to those who couldn't hear it before. In the end, he's finally heard.

This narrowing and inhabiting complicates how I understood discernment. I thought the process meant choosing among good options aligned with divine will. Sonny's story suggests a flip side: that discernment begins where options end, where only one form remains. The narrowing, like so many parable paradoxes, is what makes commitment possible and more likely even. I still struggle with this logic. I understand it conceptually and for others. I've yet to experience it myself. Perhaps more honestly, I struggle with obedience. Rev. Erin joked that many of us ask God for clarity within a preset menu of options we curated ourselves. I fear I'll accurately discern God's will for me, and still refuse to inhabit it.

Richard Siken's *I Do Know Some Things* taught me a dimension of this narrowing from a different angle. Even though the prose poetry collection was removed from the syllabus and replaced due to student feedback, I still read it on my own. The book's background shows how constraint is imposed. After a stroke affected his ability to write, he moved from delineated verse into prose blocks. The external shift in text reflected his internal state, the way the best literature does. While he could no longer rely on line breaks without disorientation, he wrote in a remaining format available to him. As a longtime reader of Siken, beginning with *Crush*, the 2005 selection for the Yale Series of Younger Poets, I can attest to how forcefully his language strikes. The perfectly fitting title reminds me of sheet metal crumpling in a car crash.

I Do Know Some Things demands attention without pause and through sustained pressure. Meaning emerges through slow pacing and accumulation. I'm reminded of Pope Paul VI's plea to artists as masters in rendering the invisible world intelligible. Siken renders an interiority shaped by diminished capacity, visible for all to feel. Though my own disability is more mental than physical, I understand his work as part of a longer lineage including *The Diving Bell and the Butterfly*, a 1997 memoir detailing a journalist's life after his entire body was paralyzed except for his left eye. The film adaptation depicts him writing by blinking letters one by one. These constraints reveal a depth of dimensions in what would otherwise not appear.

Toni Morrison pushes this constraint into its most unbearable extreme in *Beloved* where the space of discernment narrows to its limit. I resonate with Sethe in a way that unsettles me. I recognize someone loving another in a way that goes tragically awry. In a central scene the novel refers to as the Misery, her actions are catastrophic, yet intentional. They make sense to her as they do to me: she reads the situation, understands the stakes, and acts. When Paul D confronts her years later, she explains it plainly:

"...How did it work?"
"They ain't at Sweet Home. Schoolteacher ain't got em."
"Maybe there's worse."
"It ain't my job to know what's worse. It's my job to know what is and to keep them away from what I know is terrible. I did that" (194).

I felt the floor drop when I read this exchange because I recognized the logic. It's the same internal coherence that makes codependency invisible to the person inside it. Sethe discerned, albeit in a split second, like the German priest Maximilian Kolbe exchanging his life for another in a Holocaust concentration camp. She chose. The field was as narrow as a field gets, and still she chose. This raises a question I don't know how to resolve: if discernment is choice, what happens when every available one is unbearable? What does it mean to act with full intention from the narrowest possible squeeze, and then to both accept and inhabit the consequences for the rest of one's life?

Of course, this question of constraint extends beyond literature, as Pope Leo also recognizes in his *Encounter with the World of Cinema* address. Some people have far more space to choose from than others, and that unevenness can feel like injustice. I've slowly started to hold room for this paradox since a wider field can produce its own paralysis. If everything is possible, nothing is necessary. I'm reminded of a line from *Challengers* (2024), when Tashi remarks that her only skill in life is hitting a ball with a racquet. The line is self-deprecating, but it hints at a truth: her narrow field made excellence possible. When injury forecloses that path permanently, what remains? She reconfigures; she becomes a tennis coach, ultimately for her star player husband, perhaps in an attempt to live out her dreams vicariously. Her narrowing, while undeniably disappointing and uncomfortable, creates the conditions for a different kind of commitment—and growth, however undesired.

In Lori Ostlund's short story, *Just Another Family*, the narrator barely mentions working as a writer, but language saturates the story as a way of remaking an upbringing we later uncover. When I read the opening page, "She was sure that I was saying *soda* to bother her because she said there was no way a person could grow up saying *pop* and then find herself one day just thinking *soda,*" I recognized a deep indignancy. Anyone who has lived inside another's alcoholism, can read those behavioral patterns without explicit statement. That literacy, reading the shape of another's life, with one's own experience is a form of empathy literature powerfully provides.

My own life has its version of constraint and narrowing, both chosen and not. With bipolar disorder, it's not *if* another mood episode will come but *when*. My stability depends on a structure that constrains but supports: medication management, monitoring, routines that anticipate rather than react. This structure is what makes my life livable. In this way, limits can serve to focus attention. They too are part of discernment.

My understanding of discernment has shifted drastically. Even the moments at St. Columba's read differently now. The breadcrumbs revealed themselves because I was already lost and looking. Discernment can happen through limitations, not simply despite them. The narrowing of circumstance is entwined with meaning-making, an opportunity. Like the design constraints in architecture, or any other creative endeavor, it's what gives beauty its shape.

Henry 磊磊 Roark is beloved. He has many identities and walks in many worlds. He enjoys reading creative nonfiction, works in translation, and/or literary fiction; writing essays; and making visual art in various media, currently origami and collage. This is his second collection.

He lives in San Francisco with his chosen family, represents SFPL Harvey Milk Memorial Branch on the Council for Neighborhood Libraries, and serves on the Board of Directors at the historic Roxie Theater. You can get lost on his desktop at henryroark.com.